Contents

Acknowledgments

Preface

Introduction

Conversion Tables

Soda Breads & Scones   1

Hot off the Griddle   18

Tea Breads, Bracks & Buns   29

Yeast Breads   40

Speciality Breads   53

Cakes & Biscuits   65

Pastry & Puddings   82

Festive Fare   97

Useful information   120

Ingredients   120

Basic Recipes   125

Index

For my parents, Jean and Brian Campbell —
the greatest bakers of them all

Acknowledgments

Thanks are due to an enormous number of people for their help with this book. First, of course, special thanks go to all the dedicated cooks from all over Ireland who have generously shared their recipes — and their time — with me. Visiting them, sampling their delicious creations and talking about them has been a great privilege. These, and the growing number of other like-minded cooks, are the people who are keeping the great Irish baking tradition alive and taking it into a new and exciting phase.

On the production side, thanks to the team at Wolfhound Press, especially my editors Susan Houlden and Roberta Reeners and publisher Seamus Cashman. And then there's that genius with the camera — Rai Uhlemann has once again come up with wonderful photographs from all over the country and I am grateful for his enthusiasm as much as his skill. Thanks also to the designer Brenda Dermody for bringing the words to life.

Needless to say, we are all very grateful to Shamrock Foods for their sponsorship, support and enthusiasm for the project.

Finally, thanks go to my family for their (usually) good-humoured tolerance of domestic upheaval during the writing stage of this book!

The Best of Irish Breads & Baking

Traditional, Contemporary & Festive

Georgina Campbell

WOLFHOUND PRESS

First published in 1996 by
Wolfhound Press
68 Mountjoy Square
Dublin 1, Ireland

Wolfhound Press receives financial assistance from the Arts Council/An Comhairle
Ealaíonn, Dublin.

British Library Cataloguing in Publication Data
A catalogue for this book is available from the British Library.

ISBN: 0-86327-500-1

Editorial consultant: Roberta Reeners
Cover photograph: Rai Uhlemann
Cover design: Slick Fish
Design & Typesetting: Brenda Dermody at Estresso
Index compiled by Helen Litton
Printed in Ireland by Colour Books

Preface

My earliest memories are of baking. My mother, her sleeves rolled up and apron dusty with flour, rolling out pastry at the scrubbed table in our farmhouse kitchen. The warm, yeasty smell of my father's bread rising on the back of the Aga, with my favourite cat — a tamed wild tabby called simply Granny Cat — stationed firmly in front of it.

As the autumn evenings drew in, dried fruit was sorted and washed, then spread out on trays over the Aga to dry out before the Christmas baking could begin. The warm, sweet scent of fruit from distant countries permeated the house, mingling with a child's thoughts of Christmas to inspire dreams of the Bible lands, with their white-washed, flat-roofed houses seen against deep blue skies.

Schooling somehow mingled with these memories too. I can still see my mother pausing for a moment to write a word in 'joined-up writing' for me to copy. That word was 'cook' and, looking back, it has often seemed a strangely significant moment — already happiest surrounded by the paraphernalia of family cooking, perhaps my future as a food writer was sealed at that moment.

My mother is a Scotswoman, incidentally, and 'Domestic Science' trained, so it's no wonder I identify so strongly with the baking tradition in Ireland which, especially in the North, shares so much with the Scots — or that one of my favourite cookery writers should be Florence Irwin, who trained in Edinburgh at the famous College of Domestic Science at Atholl Crescent.

Baking is often referred to as therapeutic, and indeed it is. Baking will not be rushed, and the certainty of its time-honoured rhythms provides a constant background of reality in the confusion of our fast-changing lives. The warm feelings it induces in people are more than simple nostalgia or sentimentality: it reminds us of the fundamental truth, that hearth and home are vital to our well-being and health, giving us a true sense of purpose in life.

These memories from my childhood are the kind most of us would like for our own children. And although we cannot get away from the fact that times have changed (and not necessarily for the worse), the basic values implied need not be a thing of the past. Whether of necessity or for recreation, the simple, timeless pleasures and rewards of home baking are there for everyone.

Georgina Campbell.

September 1996

Introduction

*'Modern transport which brings the baker's van daily to all doors has not yet
quite ousted the home-made soda and wheaten bread which is universally made
and eaten all over Ireland.'*   Florence Irwin, 1949

The seeds of this book were sown in the 1980s when I was working on a
traditional cookery book, *Good Food from Ireland*. The baking chapters took on a
life of their own and had to be cut back drastically — the whole area was
fascinating and I realised then that there was a book on Irish breads and baking
just trying to get out. The 'yeasts had been activated' and, far from losing interest
once it was finished, my enthusiasm for expanding those early bread chapters has
been growing steadily ever since — and, although that book is now out of print, a
few of the recipes used in it have found their way into these pages.

The quotation above from Florence Irwin's classic *The Cookin' Woman* should give
us all great hope. The baker's van may have been and gone, the supermarket shelves
may now be stacked with sliced pans/loaves — but, nearly half a century later, the
home-made sodas and wheaten breads have most emphatically not been ousted!

Home baking is now one of the greatest strengths of Irish cooking. At a time
when it has declined to the point of being almost non-existent in many other
countries, excellence of baking is becoming a trademark for Irish cooks, and it's
the simple pleasures — like biting into a piece of crusty, freshly baked soda bread,
still warm from the oven and thickly spread with melting butter and home-made
jam — which visitors to Ireland find so memorable. A high proportion of our
baking is traditional to the country although, of course, outside influences have
played a role in the development of baking, as with Irish food in general. The
famous 'country house style' owes a great deal to English cookery and, in the
north of Ireland especially, a strong Scottish influence dates back at least as far as
the early seventeenth century and is particularly reflected in the great baking
tradition of the northern counties.

Traditional baking has never been appreciated more than it is now. Soda breads
and scones, griddle bakes like potato breads, Boxty and pancakes, farmhouse cakes,
bracks and tea breads of every description are filling professional kitchens and (to a
lesser extent, perhaps) private kitchens all over Ireland with the deliciously warm
and evocative aromas that are the essence of baking — and everyone, Irish resident
and visitor alike, is relishing the experience.

Not only is traditional Irish baking thriving, but the growing general interest in baking has encouraged cooks in Ireland to be more adventurous and experiment with other non-native styles. There has never been a tradition of yeast baking in Ireland, for example, as all truly traditional Irish cooking relates to the fact that everything was cooked over an open fire until relatively recently — a method which was ideally suited to the ingredients that were easily available to make unleavened breads, potato cakes, pancakes and oatcakes and, with buttermilk and (from the early nineteenth century) bread soda as leavening agents, also soda breads and griddle scones.

About 250 years ago, iron ranges began to appear in the 'big houses' of the gentry and then gradually made their way into prosperous farmhouses. But the 3-legged pot and all the skills associated with cooking at the hearth were still very much in use in some areas until well into the twentieth century. Roasting and baking were done in flat-bottomed, 3-legged 'pot-ovens' or 'bastibles' — one of which would be kept exclusively for bread-making — which were designed to take hot turves on the lid and so give an all-round heat. Flat-bottomed skillets and frying pans were set on a trivet, as were small, long-handled pans and 'mullers' which were used for heating liquids and drinks. Griddles were kept in several sizes for making scones, potato bread and other griddle bakes, and spit-roasting was also quite common.

It is interesting to reflect on the reasons why home baking declined less dramatically in Ireland than in neighbouring European countries during the difficult middle years of this century — and why it is enjoying such a strong revival today. The reasons for its survival include the fact that, in a mainly agricultural economy, home-baked bread remained central to national eating habits for much longer than in more industrialised societies. Also, soda breads are particularly quick and easy to make. Yet, although the excellence of bread is the basic strength of Irish baking, biscuits, scones and especially cakes are also a cause for pride; it has always been seen as essential to have a good selection on the farmhouse kitchen table for supper.

Now, this style of eating is also finding favour with those discerning visitors to Ireland who are most appreciative of the good home baking which makes farmhouse and country house accommodation an increasingly attractive option. Add to this the effects of a widespread revival of interest in regional cuisines and it becomes clear why we have such a vibrant interest in traditional baking.

Although baking with yeast was regarded with suspicion until quite recently by the majority of Irish cooks (who thought, understandably, that it was an unnecessarily lengthy process and generally 'difficult', an accurate enough assessment, since native Irish wheat is too 'soft' for successful yeast cookery), events have conspired to reverse this view over the last decade or so. 'Strong' bakers' flour became more easily available and, crucially, there was the arrival of the new 'easy-blend' dried yeast which encouraged cooks who were totally inexperienced in yeast cookery to have a go. Once it proved to be both easy and reliable, there was no turning back. Indeed, once confidence was established, many people started thinking about using fresh yeast and found it a wonderfully rewarding experience. From there it was but a short step towards making the wide range of speciality breads that are currently so popular in restaurants and bakeries all over the country — and which have now broadened our choice of delicious, freshly baked goods to an extent that would have been unimaginable even a decade ago.

It is said that 'cooking is a fine art, but an imprecise science'. This is certainly true of baking, which is such a personal thing that no two people using the same recipe are likely to produce identical results. In soda bread and scone making, this is usually to do with lightness of touch — the flour needs to be lifted and aerated, any fat rubbed in lightly with the finger tips, then the liquid mixed in quickly and decisively with a knife so that the dough retains as much elasticity as possible. Another factor is the natural absorbency of flour which affects the quantity of liquid required in any recipe. This will vary, not only according to type but also to storage conditions and, quite literally, depending on the weather. So it's essential to be sensitive to the variables and use common sense when baking. Being a good baker is traditionally a point of honour in Ireland. It is not only extremely satisfying, but there's no easier way to impress family and friends with your skills as a cook than by presenting them with a crusty home-baked loaf or a batch of scones warm from the oven. It's the oldest form of hospitality known, and still the finest.

What a happy coincidence that these gentle, timeless kitchen skills also provide the perfect antidote to the stresses and strains of today's competitive, 'instant' world. There has never been a better time to bring together the old and new traditions of baking. Through this book, I hope that a new generation will learn to love the unhurried rhythm of kneading, proving and knocking back, the aromas that pervade the house, the satisfaction of making good things which will give pleasure to others — all of which add up to as rewarding an activity as could be imagined.

Conversion Tables

Weight

The Imperial pound (lb) = 450g (approx.), slightly less than ½ kilogram (500g).

Imperial	Metric	Imperial	Metric
1 oz	25g	10 oz	275g
2 oz	50g	12 oz	325-350g
3 oz	75g	14 oz	400g
4 oz	100-125g	1 lb (16 oz)	450g
5 oz	150g	1½ lb	700g
6 oz	175g	2 lb	900g
7 oz	200g	3 lb	1.4 kg
8 oz	225g		

Liquid Capacity

The Imperial pint = 20 fl oz, slightly more than ½ litre (approx. 575 ml).
The American pint (see below) = 16 fl oz.

Imperial	Metric	Imperial	Metric
1 fl oz	25 ml	8 fl oz	225 ml
2 fl oz	50 ml	9 fl oz	250 ml
3 fl oz	75 ml	10 fl oz (½ pint)	275-300 ml
4 fl oz	100-125 ml	15 fl oz (¾ pint)	425 ml
5 fl oz	150 ml	20 fl oz (1 pint)	575-600 ml
6 fl oz	175 ml	30 fl oz (1½ pint)	850 ml
7 fl oz	200 ml	40 fl oz	1.15 litre

Oven Temperatures

°F	°C	Gas	°F	°C	Gas
250	130	1/2	375	190	5
275	140	1	400	200	6
300	150	2	425	210-220	7
325	160-170	3	450	230	8
350	180	4	475	240	9

A Guide for American Users
1 US cup liquid = 8 fl oz/225 ml
1 US pint = 16 fl oz/2 ½ cups
Flour: 1 US cup = 150g/4 oz. 1 lb (16 oz) = 4 cups
Caster and granulated sugar: 1 US cup = 225g/8 oz
Caster and granulated sugar: 1 level tbsp = 25g/1 oz
Brown sugar: 1 US cup = 170g/6 oz
Butter/margarine/lard: 1 US cup = 225g/8 oz (¼ lb = ¼ stick)
Sultanas (dried green grapes)/raisins: 1⅓ US cups = 225g/8 oz
Currants: 1 US cup = 150g/5 oz
Ground almonds: 1⅓ US cups = 225/g/8 oz
Golden (Karo) syrup: 1 US cup = 340g/12 oz

Soda Breads & Scones

Of all the baking that delights the traveller in Ireland, it's the simple, traditional soda breads that make the most impact. Every hotel, restaurant and guesthouse has its own 'house' recipe, baked fresh every day. Where professional hospitality is concerned, the quality — and variety — of fresh home baking is a real point of pride.

It is amazing to see the great variety of recipes for brown soda breads. Although they may look similar at first glance, each has travelled its own special route to become the unique product of a particular house. Just compare them and see how they vary in those crucial details that affect the character of the loaf.

Traditional brown soda breads are formed into rounds and marked deeply with a cross to ensure even cooking. Some are baked on greased and floured baking sheets, while others are baked in loaf tins. A few are baked in casseroles with lids — the most traditional method of all, as it is the closest to cooking in the old 'bastible' cast-iron ovens once used over the open fire with hot turves piled on top to give all-round heat.

The most crucial ingredient in bread-making is the flour. (See pages 122-3 for the characteristics of different types of flour.) Coarse wholemeal (whole-wheat) flour — whether on its own or blended with a finer type or with a plain white flour to make a lighter textured loaf — is the most common and traditional. However, there are countless variations, both old and new. Not only wheat but also barley, rye and oats each hold an important position in the development of bread-making in Ireland.

Bread and cheese form a special partnership, so it may not be a coincidence that the small-scale production of both has seen an extraordinary renaissance over the last twenty years. The success of farmhouse cheeses seems to have acted as a catalyst, encouraging other small producers as well as changing attitudes to food generally. It continues to play an important role in developing a deeper appreciation of the good food Ireland has to offer.

Many Irish bread recipes include mixed grains. In modern recipes, this may be due to the current fashions, as well as reflecting a willingness to experiment. Historically, it was often a question of necessity and availability, with pulses such as dried peas and lentils being ground into a meal and making a palatable 'cake'. An unusual grain that played an important role for a hundred years or so was Indian corn or yellow meal (called 'yalla male' in the North). Imported from America in great quantities to relieve distress during the famines of the nineteenth century, it was usually mixed with other grains to make a wholesome, distinctive yellow bread. Florence Irwin's recipe for Indian Meal Scones, published in 1949, is passed on here as a curiosity.

Another factor affecting the style of any loaf is the amount and type of raising agent. Bicarbonate of soda (bread/baking soda), in combination with buttermilk, is generally used — and the most common fault in Irish bread is using too much soda, to the detriment of flavour, colour and texture.

Buttermilk, another traditional ingredient, varies considerably in quality and is not always available. It can be made quite easily, however, using a yeast starter to create a buttermilk 'plant', known as 'winter buttermilk' in the country because it could be used until supplies of fresh milk increased with the new grass in the spring. Starting a buttermilk plant is an intriguing process and well worth trying if regular access to ordinary buttermilk is a problem.

Whether making bread or scones, many additional ingredients can change the character of the original recipe dramatically. Both savoury and sweet, they range from fruit to herbs and cheeses, seeds such as caraway, sunflower, poppy and sesame, and spices such as saffron.

Make your own buttermilk plant

Buttermilk is an essential ingredient in traditional soda breads. The lactic acid in the buttermilk reacts with the bread/baking soda (sodium bicarbonate), creating gases that make the dough rise. The reaction is very quick, so it is important to have a hot oven ready and to bake the bread at once before the gas escapes.

Buttermilk can be cultured quite easily using a buttermilk plant. This version is adapted and updated from Florence Irwin's 1949 recipe.

¾ pint/450 ml/2 cups skimmed milk
¼ pint/150 ml/½ cup boiling water
1 oz/25g yeast
2 tsp/2½ US tsp sugar

Heat the milk to lukewarm by adding the boiling water. Then add the yeast and sugar. Pour into a sterilised screw-top jar, allowing enough head space for the contents to be shaken. Place the jar on its side in a warm, dark place (an airing cupboard is perfect). Shake several times a day for 4-6 days, depending on the temperature, while the buttermilk plant is forming. Then remove the jar and open it carefully to prevent it bubbling over. Strain the contents into a jug — the cultured sour milk in the jug is used as buttermilk. The lumpy bits of yeast left in the strainer can be washed and re-used indefinitely. As the plant grows, it can be divided to share with others.

To re-use

Pour lukewarm water through the bits left in the strainer and wash off all remaining milk. Return the yeast (the buttermilk plant) to the washed and scalded jar, adding lukewarm milk and water as before. Repeat the ripening process, straining again after about 4 days (maybe 2 days in summer) when it is sour and thick.

At the end of each day, any leftover milk can be added to the jar if there is room.

Always wash all the old milk from the yeast and make sure that the jar is properly sterilised before starting another brew.

Alternatives

*Although the results are not quite the same, **yogurt** is sometimes mixed with sweet (fresh) milk and works in a way which is similar to buttermilk.
***Cream of tartar** can be added to the dry ingredients to provide the acid.
***Sweet milk** can be soured by adding lemon juice.

Breads

Basic Brown Soda Bread

This simple, wholesome bread can be eaten fresh with butter, farmhouse cheese and a bowl of home-made soup, or some crisp sticks of celery. It slices better if left to cool and 'set' for at least 4 hours. Makes l large loaf.

> l lb/450g/4 cups coarse wholemeal (whole-wheat) flour
> 6 oz/175g/1½ cups plain white (all-purpose) flour
> l rounded tsp/1¼ US tsp bread (baking) soda
> l tsp/1¼ US tsp salt
> ¾ pint/450 ml/2 cups buttermilk (approx.)

Preheat a hot oven, 400°F/200°C/gas 6.

Mix the dry ingredients in a mixing bowl. Stir in enough buttermilk to make a fairly soft dough. Turn onto a work surface dusted with wholemeal (whole-wheat) flour and knead lightly until smooth underneath. Form into a circle, about 1 ½ "/4 cm thick, and put onto a baking sheet. Mark a deep cross in the top with a floured knife. Bake for about 45 minutes, until the bread is browned and sounds hollow when tapped on the base. Cool on a wire rack, wrapped in a clean tea/dish towel to keep the crust soft.

Bee's Brown Bread

A speciality at Tinakilly House near Wicklow since William and Bee Power opened it to guests in 1983. Although the ingredients have been modernised, the cooking method is one of the most traditional as it is baked in a casserole with a lid, much as the old cast-iron 'bastible' was used over an open fire. Keeps relatively well although it contains no fat. Makes 1 loaf.

> 13 oz/375g/3⅓ cups coarse ground wholemeal (whole-wheat) flour
> 7 oz/200g/1¾ cups self-raising flour
> l tsp/1¼ US tsp salt
> l tsp/1¼ US tsp bread (baking) soda
> l tbsp/1¼ US tbsp brown sugar
> ¾ pint/450 ml/2 cups buttermilk

Preheat a fairly hot oven, 400°F/200°C/gas 6. Grease a 2-pint/1.2 litre casserole.

Mix all the dry ingredients together with a knife, then mix in the buttermilk. Combine thoroughly but *do not knead*. Turn the mixture into the prepared casserole, cover with a lid and bake in the centre of the oven for 1 hour. When ready, the bread will shrink slightly from the side of the casserole and will sound hollow when turned out and tapped on the base. Cool on a wire rack. If you like a soft crust, wrap the loaf in a clean tea/dish towel to cool.

Grandmother's Bread

Le Coq Hardi is a very classy Dublin restaurant, renowned for the excellence of chef-patron John Howard's classic French cooking as well as for delicious details such as their gorgeous brown bread. Although this moist, dark, richly flavoured mixed-grain loaf seems quite modern, it is actually a recipe from Catherine Howard's grandmother and dates back to the turn of the century. Makes 2 large loaves.

> 1½ lb/700g/6 cups wheaten meal
> 8 oz/225g/2 cups plain (all-purpose) flour
> 2 oz/50g/2 US tbsp wheat bran
> 2 oz/50g/⅓ cup pinhead oatmeal
> 1 tsp/1¼ US tsp salt
> 1 tsp/1¼ US tsp bread (baking) soda
> 2 tsp/2½ US tsp soft brown sugar (approx.)
> 1 tbsp/1¼ US tbsp treacle (molasses),
>   dissolved in about 2 oz/50g/½ stick melted butter
> 1½ pints/900 ml/3¾ cups buttermilk (approx.)

Preheat a very hot oven, 450°F/230°C/gas 8. Oil two 2 lb/900g loaf tins.

Mix all dry ingredients thoroughly. Then add the treacle/molasses and butter mixture and enough buttermilk to make a very wet dough. Turn into the oiled tins and bake for 15 minutes. Reduce the heat to 300°F/150°C/gas 2 for another hour, until the loaves sound hollow when turned out and tapped on the base. Cool on a wire rack.

Ballylickey Wheaten Bread

Formal gardens provide a lovely frame for sweeping views of Bantry Bay from Ballylickey Manor House. It is now run as a small hotel by George Graves, nephew of the poet Robert, who was once a frequent visitor. Although George is a francophile, this doesn't interfere with his appreciation of the simple goodness of things Irish. As proof, he gave me his recipe for this toothsome loaf which is quick and easy to make. Exact quantities are unimportant as long as the proportions are right. Makes 1 loaf.

> 2 large tbsp plain (all-purpose) flour
> 5   tbsp wheaten (whole-wheat) flour
> 1 large tbsp bran
> 1 large tbsp wheat germ
> 1 heaped tsp bread (baking) soda
> pinch of salt
> buttermilk, as required

Preheat a hot oven, 400°F/200°C/gas 6.

Mix all the dry ingredients in a bowl and filter through the fingers to aerate. Mix in enough buttermilk to moisten well. Turn out onto a floured board and shape as required. The traditional round, cut deeply with a cross for even baking, is hard to beat. It can also be turned into a greased loaf tin. Bake for 30 minutes, until the loaf is well-risen with a crisp crust. The base should sound hollow when rapped with the knuckles. Cool on a wire rack and use on the day of baking.

Newport House Brown Bread

A visit to Newport House, Co. Mayo, is one of the joys of travelling in the north-west. Although the cuisine is sophisticated, the simple things in life are also valued. Chef John Gavin bakes this delicious bread for the lunch-time picnic hampers — it goes particularly well with their home-smoked salmon. The butter gives it an especially good flavour and improves the keeping qualities — although, like all soda breads, it is best eaten on the day of baking. Makes 3 loaves.

> 3 lb/1.4 kg/12 cups plain (all-purpose) flour
> 8 oz/225g/2 cups wholemeal (whole-wheat) flour
> 6 oz/175g/1½ cups bran
> 2 level tsp/2½ US tsp bread (baking) soda
> 5 oz/150g/1¼ sticks butter
> 2½ pints/1½ litres/6¼ cups buttermilk (approx.)

Preheat a very hot oven, 450°F/230°C/gas 8.
   Put all the dry ingredients into a large bowl and mix with the hands. Cut in the butter and mix with the flours. Then quickly mix in enough milk to make a soft *but not sticky dough*. Turn out onto a floured worktop, divide into 3 pieces and knead lightly until smooth on the underside. Turn over and place on a well-floured baking tray. Cut a cross in the top to ensure even baking. Bake for about 30 minutes, until the loaves are well-risen and nicely browned. The base should sound hollow when rapped with the knuckles.

Granny Nixon's Wheaten Loaf

This light brown loaf from the North of Ireland was made regularly by my mother-in-law, who handed it on to me. It makes an unusual even-textured loaf with a thin, crisp crust and is one of the quickest to prepare as the wet mixture is simply poured into the tins for baking. A good loaf by any standards — it's moist, cuts well and keeps surprisingly well for a fat-free soda bread. Makes two 7"/18 cm round loaves.

> 12 oz/350g/3 cups fairly fine wholemeal (whole-wheat) flour
> 12 oz/350g/3 cups plain (all-purpose) flour
> 1 level tbsp/1¼ US tbsp sugar
> 2 level tsp/2½ US tsp baking (bread) soda
> ½ tsp salt
> 1 pint/600 ml/2½ cups buttermilk

Preheat a fairly hot oven, 400°F/200°C/gas 6. Grease two 7"/18 cm sandwich tins.
   Put the dry ingredients in a bowl and mix well. Then add the buttermilk and mix thoroughly to make a very wet mixture. Pour into the prepared tins and bake near the top of the oven for about ½ hour. When cooked, the loaves will shrink slightly from the sides of the tins. They will turn out easily and should be crisp on the base. Cool on a wire rack, wrapping lightly in a clean tea/dish towel if you like a softer crust.

Mary Ann's Brown Bread

Patricia O'Mahony makes this bread every day at Mary Ann's, the O'Mahonys' famous old pub in the picturesque waterside village of Castletownshend, Co. Cork. The nutty flavour of this wonderfully moist loaf is the perfect accompaniment to the delicious seafood dishes served in both the bar and restaurant. This makes a wet mixture which is simply turned into the baking tin. Makes 1 large loaf.

l lb/450g/4 cups extra coarse wholemeal (whole-wheat) flour
1 tbsp/1¼ US tbsp bran
1 tbsp/1¼ US tbsp wheat germ
1 tbsp/1¼ US tbsp pinhead oatmeal
1 tsp/1¼ US tsp salt
1 tsp/1¼ US tsp sugar
1 tsp/1¼ US tsp bread (baking) soda, sifted
1 tbsp/1¼ US tbsp oil
1 egg, lightly beaten
16 fl oz/450 ml/2 cups buttermilk (approx.)

Preheat a very hot oven, 450°F/230°C/gas 8. Grease a 2 lb/900g loaf tin.
   Mix dry ingredients well in a mixing bowl. Combine liquids and mix well with the dry ingredients to make a fairly wet dough. Turn into the prepared tin and bake for about 1 hour. Remove from the tin for the last five minutes' baking if you like a crisp crust. Cool on a wire rack.

Ashford Castle Brown Bread

This recipe is in regular use at the grandest of Ireland's castle hotels, a magical place in a most beautiful location. It is very easy to make and especially useful when buttermilk is unavailable. Makes one 8"/20 cm round loaf.

1 lb/450g/4 cups wholemeal (whole-wheat) flour
1 rounded tsp/1¼ US tsp salt
1 rounded tsp/1¼ US tsp bread (baking) soda
1 rounded tsp/1¼ US tsp cream of tartar
1-2 oz/25-50g/¼ -½ stick butter or margarine
1 tbsp/1¼ US tbsp honey
¾ pint/450 ml/2 cups milk

Preheat a very hot oven, 475°F/240°C/gas 9. Butter an 8"/20 cm sandwich tin.
   Put the flour into a mixing bowl, add the salt and sift in the bread/baking soda and cream of tartar. Mix the dry ingredients together very thoroughly. Melt the butter and honey together and mix with the milk. Make a well in the centre of the flour mixture, add all the liquid and mix together quickly but thoroughly with a knife to make a wet dough. Pour into the buttered tin and level off roughly. Put straight into the preheated oven and immediately reduce the temperature to 350°F/180°C/gas 4. Bake for about 1 hour, until the loaf is well-risen, nicely browned and shrinking slightly from the tin. Turn out of the tin for the last five minutes' baking and turn upside down to crisp up the base. Cool on a wire rack and use fresh on the day of baking, if possible.

St Ernans Mixed Grain & Yogurt Loaf

This is typical of the food served at this hauntingly peaceful place on its own island just outside Donegal town. It is simple and wholesome, the perfect accompaniment to home-made soup, marmalade or jam. A lovely nutty bread, the ingredients suggest a curious mixture of baking traditions. The use of mixed grains in Irish baking is a legacy of necessity in times of hardship, so this recipe is especially appropriate to the place: in the last century, grateful tenants built the causeway to the island as a gesture of thanks to a kind and generous landlord. Makes 2 small loaves.

12 oz/350g/3 cups coarse wholemeal (whole-wheat) flour
12 oz/350g/3 cups plain white (all-purpose) flour
2 oz/50g/½ stick butter or margarine
2 tbsp/2½ US tbsp sunflower seeds
2 tbsp/2½ US tbsp pinhead oatmeal
1 oz/25g/1 US tbsp brown sugar
1 tsp/1¼ US tsp salt
1 tsp/1¼ US tsp cream of tartar
1 tsp/1¼ US tsp baking (bread) soda
1 tsp/1¼ US tsp baking powder
5 fl oz/150 ml/½ cup natural yogurt
10 fl oz/300 ml/1¼ cups milk (approx.)

Preheat a very hot oven, 425°F/220°C/gas 7. Grease and flour two 1 lb/450g loaf tins.

Place the flours in a bowl and rub in the butter or margarine until the mixture resembles fine breadcrumbs. Then add all the remaining dry ingredients, reserving a teaspoon each of sunflower seeds and oatmeal for sprinkling on top. Mix thoroughly. Make a well in the centre, then add the yogurt and enough milk to make a soft dough. Divide in two, knead lightly and place in the prepared tins. Sprinkle the reserved seeds on top and bake for 40-45 minutes, until the bread sounds hollow when tapped on the base. Turn out of the tins and cool on a wire rack.

Wheaten Bread

Reg Ryan and Phil McAfee run the highly regarded Restaurant St John's at Fahan on Lough Swilly. Phil's bread sets the tone for a relaxing evening of good food and conversation. With a high fat content, it is a rich, moist mixture in the tradition of the old Northern 'Butter Cakes' which keeps better than most soda breads. Delicious eaten warm from the oven. Makes 5 small (1 lb/450g) loaves.

1¼ lb/475g/5 cups coarse wholemeal (whole-wheat) flour
1¼ lb/475g/5 cups medium wholemeal (whole-wheat) flour
3 oz/75g/3 US tbsp sugar
1 heaped tsp/1¼ US tsp baking soda
10 oz/275g/1¼ cups soft margarine
2 pints/1.2 litres/5 cups buttermilk (approx.)

Preheat a hot oven, 425°F/220°C/gas 7. Oil five 1 lb/450g loaf tins.

Put all dry ingredients into a mixing bowl. Rub in margarine. Add enough milk to make a *soft but not sticky* consistency. Divide the mixture into 5 pieces and place each one on a board dusted with coarse wholemeal (whole-wheat) flour. Toss the mixture in the flour, working very lightly. Place in the well-oiled loaf tins. Make a cross on the top of each and bake for 1 hour. Turn onto a wire rack and cover with a clean tea/dish towel to cool.

Lovett's White Soda Bread

Although brown soda bread is more widely made and with many variations, a good white soda bread is something else. It is lighter in texture and more delicate in flavour, demanding a perfect balance of ingredients. When everything comes together, it is a treat indeed, though more likely to be found in Northern Ireland than farther south. Except perhaps at Lovett's. This is one of Cork city's longest established restaurants, famous for the quality of Margaret's food and Dermod's easy hospitality. A memorable culinary highlight at Lovett's is Margaret's bread, a fat-free recipe with a light, moist texture and a crisp crust. Makes 3 large loaves.

> 2 lb/900g/8 cups plain white (all-purpose) flour
> 2 level tsp/2½ US tsp bread (baking) soda, sifted
> 1 tsp/1¼ US tsp salt
> 1½ -2 pints/900-1200 ml/4-5 cups buttermilk (as required)

Preheat a hot oven, 400°F/200°C/gas 6. Grease three 2 lb/900g loaf tins.

Mix the dry ingredients well in a large mixing bowl. Then, mixing with the hands, add enough buttermilk to make a fairly moist dough. Turn out onto a floured surface, knead lightly and divide between the three tins. (Alternatively, shape into the traditional rounds, cut a cross into the top and bake on a greased baking sheet.) Bake for about 20 minutes, by which time the loaves should have risen to the top of the tins. Then turn out of the tins and cook for a further 10-15 minutes, until the crust is golden-brown and the base sounds hollow when tapped. Cool on a wire rack and use very fresh.

Mitchell's Brown Soda Bread with Seeds

Jerry and Margaret Mitchell's restaurant is in a lovely old cut-stone building high in the Wicklow Hills at Laragh, near Glendalough. Margaret makes this wonderful bread both to serve at the restaurant and for sale. It's quite a curiosity because the soda reacts with the sunflower seeds, turning them bright green, like seaweed. The intensity of the colour deepens with the amount of soda used, so it's easy to tell when the soda spoon is being over-used. Nothing is measured at Mitchell's — this is an authorised version of their daily bread, which they make in a Magimix. Makes 3 loaves.

> 8 oz/225g/2 cups wholemeal (whole-wheat) flour
> 8 oz/225g/2 cups self-raising flour
> 1 tsp bread (baking) soda
> pinch of salt
> 1 cup bran
> 1 cup wheat germ
> ½ cup each: pinhead oatmeal, jumbo oat flakes, sunflower seeds, sesame seeds
> 1 egg
> 1 pint/600 ml/2½ cups buttermilk
> 1 cup water (approx.)

Preheat a fairly hot oven, 375°F/190°C/gas 5. Grease and flour 3 loaf tins.

Put all the ingredients in a food processor and mix until thoroughly blended. Then divide between the three prepared tins. Bake for about 45 minutes, until crisp and hollow-sounding when tapped on the base. Cool on a wire rack.

Ken Buggy's Famous Brown Bread

This recipe, from one of Ireland's most respected bread-makers, regularly delights visitors to the Glencairn Inn near the magical town of Lismore, Co. Waterford. It demonstrates perfectly both the versatility ('You don't have to be exact with the amounts of flour, varying the proportions of white to brown as you like') and the immediacy of the procedure for making traditional soda bread ('. . .instantly put bread soda away'). Quantities are not given in the usual way — in the old country tradition, it is presumed that each baker will have his or her own measures which will be re-used each time. Ken even lists 'The Reasons Why Bread Fails':

*Oven not pre-heated
*Forgot to put in bread (baking) soda
*Dough kneaded too much
*Not left in oven long enough

plain white/cream (all-purpose) flour
bread (baking) soda
wholemeal (whole-wheat) flour
cream
buttermilk

Preheat a hot oven, 425°F/220°C/gas 7.

Have ready a large mixing bowl, a knife, a wooden spoon, a small sieve, a teaspoon, a floured baking tray and a teacup.

Put 3 teacups of plain white (all-purpose) flour into the mixing bowl (any size cup will do). Add 1 cup of wholemeal flour and 1 rounded teaspoon bread soda through the sieve and instantly put bread soda away. Set aside the teaspoon and sieve.

Blend the ingredients together with the wooden spoon — a few turns with the spoon is all that's needed. Add in ½ teacup of cream (leftover cream, whipped or otherwise, can be used up this way if you like) and a small carton of buttermilk — enough, when turned for a second with the wooden spoon and then mixed with the knife, to make a soft dough that is only just dry enough to come away from the bowl without being sticky.

Using clean hands, form a ball with a smooth top and flat bottom — avoid over-handling.

Reduce the oven temperature to 400°F/200°C/gas 6. Put the loaf onto the baking tray and use the knife to cut almost right through, into quarters. Bake three-quarters of the way up in the oven for 30 minutes. Then turn over and cook upside down for a further 5 minutes. The bread must have a very hard outer crust on both sides. Allow to stand upside down for at least 15 minutes.

Note: No two ovens are the same.
No two cups are the same.
No two teaspoons are the same.

Scones

Scones are usually made in the proportion of about four parts flour to one of fat. The raising agent is most often baking powder, with sweet milk to mix. When it comes to Irish baking, however, the rules are there to be broken and there are countless variations on this simple mixture.

One basic rule does apply, however — like soda breads, any delay between mixing and baking is disastrous. Whether they are destined for the oven or a hot griddle, scones need the sharp shock of heat immediately after mixing if they are to be high and light.

Traditional Plain Scones

This simple recipe makes about 8 scones.

> 8 oz/225g/2 cups plain (all-purpose) flour
> pinch of salt
> 1 rounded tsp/1¼ US tsp baking powder
> 1½ - 2 oz/40-50g/½ stick butter or margarine
> ¼ pint/150 ml/½ cup milk (approx.)
> a little beaten egg or milk, to glaze (optional)

Preheat a very hot oven, 450°F/230°C/gas 8.

Sift the dry ingredients into a mixing bowl. Cut in the butter or margarine and rub it in to make a mixture like fine breadcrumbs. Make a well in the centre and add enough milk to make a soft dough which is just firm enough to handle. Turn out onto a floured worktop and knead lightly into shape. Roll or pat out with the hand to a thickness of about 1"/2.5 cm. Stamp out rounds (1½ -2"/4-5 cm) with a floured cutter, or cut into squares or triangles with a sharp knife. Lay the scones on a floured baking sheet. Glaze them with a little beaten egg or milk, if you like. Bake for about 7-10 minutes, until brown and well-risen.

Variations

*Buttermilk or sour milk can be used instead of sweet milk, in which case baking soda is used instead of baking powder.

*Self-raising flour can be used with sweet milk, with the addition of about ½ tsp baking powder.

*Traditional Rich Tea Scones are made in the same way. Add 1-2 oz/25-50g/ 1-2 US tbsp caster (superfine) sugar with the dry ingredients. Use a beaten egg plus 1 or 2 tbsp of milk or water to mix.

*Fruit Scones need less sugar. Include about 2 oz/50g/½ cup currants, raisins, sultanas (dried green grapes) or chopped dried dates with the dry ingredients.

Buttermilk Scones

These lovely light scones can be varied to make Wheatmeal Scones — use half white and half fine wholemeal (whole-wheat) flour. Make Sultana/Raisin Scones by adding 2-4 oz/50-100g/½ -1 cup sultanas (dried green grapes) along with the sugar. Makes about 12 large scones or 18 small ones.

> 1 lb/450g/4 cups plain (all-purpose) flour
> ½ tsp salt
> 1 tsp/1¼ US tsp bread (baking) soda
> 2 oz/50g/½ stick butter, at room temperature
> 1 tbsp/1¼ US tbsp granulated sugar
> 1 small egg, lightly beaten
> ½ pint/300 ml/1¼ cups buttermilk (approx.)

Preheat a hot oven, 425°F/220°C/gas 7. Grease 2 baking trays.

Sift the flour, salt and soda into a mixing bowl. Cut in the butter and rub in until the mixture resembles fine breadcrumbs. Add the sugar and mix well. Make a well in the middle and add the egg and enough buttermilk to make a soft dough. Turn onto a floured work surface and knead lightly into shape. Roll out to about ½ "/1.2 cm thick. Cut out 12 large or 18 small scones using a fluted cutter, gathering the trimmings and lightly re-rolling as necessary. Arrange on the baking trays, leaving space between the scones. Bake for 15-20 minutes, until well-risen and golden-brown, turning the trays around halfway through the baking. Cool on wire racks and serve very fresh with butter and home-made jam.

Traditional Cheese Scones

Because of the higher fat content, a little more baking powder is needed to give a good lift to these cheese scones. Use a sharp cheese if possible for the best flavour; the mustard gives it added piquancy. Makes 8-10.

> 8 oz/225g/2 cups plain (all-purpose) flour
> 1 heaped tsp/1¼ US tsp baking powder
> 2 oz/50g/½ stick butter or margarine
> 4 oz/100g/1¼ cups hard cheese (mature Cheddar), finely grated
> 1 tsp/1¼ US tsp mustard powder or crushed mustard seeds
> a little salt
> a grinding of fresh pepper
> 4 fl oz/100 ml/½ cup milk (approx.)

Preheat a very hot oven, 450°F/230°C/gas 8.

Sift flour and baking powder into a mixing bowl. Cut in the butter or margarine and rub in to make a mixture like fine breadcrumbs. Mix in the grated cheese, mustard and seasoning. Make a well in the centre, then add the milk and mix to make a soft dough. Turn out onto a floured work surface and knead lightly. Roll out to ¾"/2 cm thick and mark into 8-10 triangles. (Alternatively, cut into rounds with a 2"/5 cm fluted cutter, or cut into squares.) Brush lightly with milk and place on a greased baking sheet. Bake for about 10-15 minutes, until well-risen and golden-brown. Use on the day of baking or, if crisped in the oven, for breakfast the following morning.

Oatmeal Scones

Oatmeal is one of Ireland's great traditional foods and is now appreciated more than ever. These delicious scones are at their best eaten warm, with good salty butter — to accompany a hearty soup or a breakfast of rashers/bacon slices and eggs. If not eaten on the day of baking, try them for making toasted cheese, using a well-flavoured farmhouse cheese. Makes 8.

6 oz/175g/1½ cups wholemeal (whole-wheat) flour
2 oz/50g/⅓ cup fine pinhead oatmeal
1 rounded tsp/1¼ US tsp bread (baking) soda
good pinch of salt
2 oz/50g/¼ cup white fat or dripping (lard)
¼ pint/150 ml/½ cup buttermilk (approx.)
milk or beaten egg and extra oatmeal, to finish

Preheat a very hot oven, 450°F/230°C/gas 8.

Mix the dry ingredients well, then rub in the fat. Make a well in the middle and mix in enough buttermilk to make a fairly soft dough. Mix thoroughly but lightly. Turn out onto a floured work surface and knead lightly. Roll or flatten out to make a rectangle about ¾"/2 cm thick and cut with a knife to make 8 squares. Brush the tops with a little beaten egg or milk and sprinkle lightly with pinhead oatmeal. Lay on a greased baking sheet and bake for 8-10 minutes, until well-risen and browned.

Oven-baked Potato Cakes

Potato cakes comes in many forms, but they're all at their best if made with freshly cooked potatoes, preferably still warm. These make an irresistible scone, eaten hot from the oven. Makes about 1 dozen.

2 oz/50g/½ stick butter
8 oz/225g/2 cups self-raising flour
½ tsp baking powder
good pinch of salt
6 oz/175g/⅔ cup mashed potato, freshly cooked
buttermilk, enough to mix

Preheat a hot oven, 425°F/220°C/gas 7.

Rub the butter into the sifted flour and baking powder and season with salt. Add the mashed potato and mix well. Incorporate enough buttermilk to make a soft dough. Turn onto a floured work surface and knead lightly. Roll out quite thickly, as for scones. Stamp out into rounds with a 2"/5 cm scone cutter, or cut into squares with a floured knife. Put onto a greased baking tray and bake for about 20 minutes, until well-risen, golden-brown and crisp. Serve straight from the oven, split open and buttered hot.

Clohamon Scones

Clohamon, the lovely family home of Sir Richard and Lady Maria Levinge, is on a working farm in Co. Wexford. It's as well known for Maria's Connemara ponies as for her wonderful cooking. They welcome guests for most of the year, but late October-early November is the unlikely high point when the annual Wexford Opera Festival is held nearby. Maria's dinners are a treat to treasure and she is an excellent, innovative baker. Her scones often feature with the soup course at dinner or freshly-baked for breakfast. Makes about 8.

8 oz/225g/2 cups strong white (bread) flour
3 level tsp/3¾ US tsp baking powder
2 tbsp/2½ US tbsp caster (superfine) sugar, or to taste
2 oz/50g/½ stick butter
scant ¼ pint/150 ml/½ cup milk

Preheat a hot oven, 425°F/210°C/gas 7.

Put all the dry ingredients and the butter into a food processor and blend to make fine crumbs. Drizzle in enough milk to make the mixture form a ball around the processing blade. Turn onto a floured board and pat into shape with your hands. Cut into rounds with a metal scone cutter and lay out on a greased baking tray. Brush the tops with a little milk and bake for 10-12 minutes, until well-risen and golden-brown.

Variations

For the many variations on these scones, no specific quantities are suggested. Individual cooks will be guided by the look and taste of the mixture.

For any of the following, process the dry ingredients and butter. Then tip the crumbed mixture into a bowl and finish by adding any of the following, plus the milk. Blend everything together with a knife.

*Sweet
Try the following: chopped walnuts; chopped cooking apple and cinnamon; sultanas (dried green grapes) and mixed spice; dried apricot and chopped almonds; natural colour glacé cherries (for afternoon tea).

*Savoury
Parmesan (or Irish Regato) and poppy seeds; grated Cheddar cheese and cayenne pepper; chilli and sun-dried tomato; almost any combination of chopped fresh garden herbs. As these are most likely to go with soup, select the herbs to complement the flavour of the soup. Mint and chives can both be lovely with cold summer soups.

Butter Scones

Especially popular in Northern areas, these are also known as Butter Cakes, since the term 'cake' has come to include other baked goods, including bread and scones. This probably originates from the griddle-baking tradition, as most baked goods (notably oatcakes) were made into rounds and referred to as 'cakes' before being divided into 'farls' (quarters). A high proportion of real butter gives this recipe a particularly good flavour and keeping qualities. Makes about 16-18.

> 1 lb/450g/4 cups flour
> good pinch of salt
> 1 level tsp/1¼ US tsp *each* bread (baking) soda and cream of tartar
>   *or* 1 heaped tsp/1¼ US tsp baking powder
> 6 oz/175g/1½ sticks butter
> 2 oz/50g/2 US tbsp caster (superfine) sugar
> ½ pint/300 ml/1¼ cups buttermilk (approx.)

Preheat a hot oven, 425°F/220°C/gas 7.

   Sift the flour, salt and raising agents into a mixing bowl. Cut in the butter and rub in lightly to make a crumbly texture. Add the sugar and mix well. Use a knife to mix in enough buttermilk to make a *soft but not wet dough*. Turn onto a floured work surface and knead very lightly. Roll out to ¾"/2 cm thick and cut into rounds with a fluted cutter. Lay on a greased baking sheet and brush the tops with a little buttermilk, if you like. Bake for about 15-20 minutes, until well-risen and golden-brown. Serve as fresh as possible with butter or cream and home-made jam, or toasted and buttered while piping hot.

Carrot & Sultana Scones

The annual Galtee *Irish Breakfast Competition* is so successful that many guesthouses now specialise in serving a breakfast good enough to carry their visitors through most of the day. Home baking is an essential ingredient, and cooks work hard to provide variety, health-consciousness and wholesomeness. At Anglesea Townhouse in Dublin, these scones provide a healthy alternative to ordinary toast on the breakfast table. Makes about 8.

> 8 oz/225g/2 cups plain (all-purpose) flour
> pinch of salt
> 1 tsp/1¼ US tsp baking powder
> 2 oz/50g/¼ cup polyunsaturated margarine
> 1 tsp/1¼ US tsp caster (superfine) sugar
> 2 oz/50g/⅓ cup sultanas (dried green grapes)
> 1 medium carrot, peeled and grated
> pinch of ground nutmeg
> 1 egg, beaten
> 2 fl oz/50 ml/¼ cup skimmed milk (approx.)

Preheat a hot oven, 400°F/200°C/gas 6.

   Sift flour, salt and baking powder into a bowl. Rub in the margarine to make a mixture like fine breadcrumbs. Mix in the remaining dry ingredients. Stir in the egg and enough milk to form a soft dough. Turn out onto a floured work surface and roll out to about ¾"/ 2 cm thick. Using a 2"/5 cm fluted cutter, cut into about 8 circles. Place on an oiled baking sheet and bake for 20-25 minutes, until well-risen and golden-brown.

James's Scones

Kealys Seafood Bar, James and Tricia Kealy's surprising little pub-cum-restaurant, is on the harbour-front in the rugged fishing port of Greencastle, way up in the north of Donegal. It's a small place with a big heart and, although seafood takes centre stage, the baking is exceptional. These scones are unusually light and often enhanced by a scattering of cheese on top — hard to resist, especially with James's superb home-made soups. Since these scones are virtually fat-free, they must be eaten very fresh — warm from the oven, if possible, but definitely on the day of baking. Makes about 30.

> 1 lb/450g/4 cups plain (all-purpose) flour
> 1 lb/450g/4 cups wheaten (whole-wheat) flour
> 1 tsp/1¼ US tsp bread (baking) soda
> 1 tsp/1¼ US tsp salt
> 24 fl oz/725 ml/scant 3 cups buttermilk (or soured cream and milk)

Preheat a hot oven, 425°F/200°C/gas 6.

Sift the plain (all-purpose) flour, soda and salt into a bowl. Add the wheaten (whole-wheat) flour and mix well. Make a well in the centre and pour in *almost all* of the liquid. Mix well with a wooden spoon, adding enough liquid to make a soft, moist dough. (*Do not over-mix.*) Dust worktop with flour and turn out dough. Dust top with flour and press out evenly to a thickness of 1½ "/3.8 cm. Cut individual scones with 2"/5 cm fluted cutter, place on an oiled and floured baking tray and brush tops with egg wash (2 egg yolks mixed with 2 tbsp water) and/or scatter with grated cheese. Bake for about 12 minutes, until well-risen and golden-brown.

Spicy Fruit Scones

Many of Ireland's finest hotels and country houses recreate that special pampered feeling of relaxation that goes with afternoon tea, served with all the trimmings and including lots of old-fashioned treats. Down in Kenmare, Co. Kerry, one of the country's most famous and beautifully located hotels aims at excellence in this delightfully civilised punctuation mark between luncheon and dinner. These are the rich, fruity scones served at the Park Hotel, Kenmare. Makes about 16.

> 1 lb/450g/4 cups plain (all-purpose) flour
> 6 oz/175g/1½ sticks butter
> 1 heaped tsp/1¼ US tsp baking powder
> 3 oz/75g/3 US tbsp sugar
> a pinch each: nutmeg, mixed spice, cinnamon
> 2 oz/50g/⅓ cup sultanas (dried green grapes)
> 2 oz/50g/⅓ cup raisins
> 2 eggs, beaten
> milk, as required

Preheat a moderate oven, 350°F/180°C/gas 4. Grease a large baking sheet.

Sift the flour into a mixing bowl. Cut in the butter and rub in until the mixture looks like fine breadcrumbs. Sprinkle in the baking powder and mix thoroughly. Add the sugar, spices and dried fruit and mix well. Make a well in the middle and add the beaten eggs and enough milk to form a soft dough. Turn out onto a floured work surface and knead lightly. When smooth, roll out lightly or flatten out with the hands to make a fairly deep round or square. Cut with a scone cutter or a knife to make round or square scones, as preferred. Lay on a greased baking sheet and brush with egg wash, if you like. Bake for 25-35 minutes, until well-risen and golden-brown.

Indian Meal Scones

Published in 1949, Florence Irwin's recipe indicates that 'yalla male' was still in use, at least in Northern Ireland, even after World War II. In some old recipes, the meal was soaked before use, in the same way as pinhead oatmeal. These were reckoned to be particularly tasty if cut into thin scone-like cakes and eaten hot with plenty of butter after baking on a griddle. Makes about 16.

> 8 oz/225g/2 cups Indian meal (corn meal/maize)
> 8 oz/225g/2 cups plain (all-purpose) flour
> ½ tsp baking (bread) soda
> ½ tsp cream of tartar
> ½ tsp salt
> 1 tbsp/1¼ US tbsp sugar
> 2 oz/50g/¼ cup lard
> buttermilk, as required

Put the meal into a basin and sift the other dry ingredients over it. Rub in the lard. Add enough buttermilk to make a dough. Knead lightly and roll out. Cut in squares or rounds and bake in a hot oven. Eat hot or cold.

Hot off the Griddle

Cast-iron ranges came into use in the 'big houses' of the gentry about 250 years ago. Their use gradually filtered down into the more prosperous 'strong' farmhouses. Meanwhile, cooking over the open fire continued well into the twentieth century. While this may seem primitive, it was actually very practical and, in skilled hands, produced surprisingly complex meals. It was far from being a simple fire with a large 'witch's cauldron' pot hanging over it. The turf fire, made on a flat stone hearth under a wide chimney, allowed for remarkable versatility, as the fire could be divided to provide heat sources for a number of simultaneous cooking processes.

Various cooking implements were suspended over the hearth. There was always a cast-iron crane mechanism on which pots of different sizes could be suspended (not only for cooking but also for laundry). There were pot-ovens for roasting and baking and, of course, griddles for frying and baking. Pot-ovens were known as 'bastibles' (perhaps because they were made in Barnstaple in Devon). One was reserved solely for bread-making and oven-baked soda breads; the lid was indented so that hot turves could be piled on top, giving an all-round heat. In addition to the daily baking of bread, skilful cooks also made all kinds of tea breads, pies and tarts in a bastible — and of course it could be used for roasting meat, hence the term 'pot roast'.

Another quite different skill was called for when using the griddle, a large round sheet of cast-iron suspended over the fire and used for griddle breads, scones, oatcakes, potato cakes, pancakes of all kinds including boxty, biscuits and 'flat-breads' or unleavened breads. Oatcakes predated other forms of bread in Ireland and were originally baked on flagstone griddles known as bake-stones. The traditional unleavened 'thin bread' was the oaten farl, shaped like a quarter circle and cooked on a hot flagstone or an iron bake-stone. The large circular 'cake' was marked with a cross so that it could be broken easily into quarters (farls) after baking. It was then hardened on a wrought-iron 'harnen stand' or 'bread-stick' toaster in front of the fire.

Although the tradition of baking on the griddle survives in some areas, modern cooks often use a heavy cast-iron frying pan, or even an electric frying pan.

Oatcakes

The most traditional of all the griddle bakes, oatcakes were originally made in big rounds, then quartered to make farls. The old method is given first, followed by variations which may be easier in modern kitchens. Makes 8-12.

> 8 oz/225g/2 cups pinhead oatmeal
> 3 oz/75g/¾ cup plain (all-purpose) flour
> good pinch of bread (baking) soda
> good pinch of salt
> 2 tbsp/2½ US tbsp bacon fat or butter, melted
> hot water
> oatmeal, to coat the work surface

Preheat a moderately hot griddle.

Measure the dry ingredients into a mixing bowl and mix well. Add the melted bacon fat or butter and blend in thoroughly. Add enough hot water to make a spongy mass — don't try to make the mixture stiff enough to roll out at this point. Scatter oatmeal thickly onto a work surface, turn the mixture onto it and scatter the top with more oatmeal. Using the back of the fingers, press the lump out into a round, keeping it dry with oatmeal on top and making sure there is always plenty underneath to prevent it from sticking.

Continue pressing out in this way until thin enough to roll. By now, it should have absorbed nearly as much oatmeal as there was in the original ingredients. Make sure there is plenty of oatmeal on the board, then roll out quite thinly with short, sharp rolls. Before cutting, scatter some fresh oatmeal on top and rub it lightly with the palm of the hand to whiten it. Then slide the whole 'cake' onto the hot griddle and mark the round into 4 farls, which can be further subdivided to make 8 or even 12 triangular biscuits. Alternatively, cut the 'cake' into individual squares or triangles. Lift onto the griddle with a palette knife and bake over a moderate heat until dried out and a pale golden-brown. Cool on a wire rack. When absolutely cold, store in an airtight tin.

Variations

Drying out can be completed under a low grill/broiler or in a cool oven, a modernised version of drying them on the 'harnen stand'. They could also be baked in a moderate oven, 350°F/180°C/gas 4, for about 40 minutes, until light brown and dry. They can also be stamped out with a biscuit/cookie cutter to make round biscuits. In all cases, maintaining a moderate temperature is important, as the oatcakes should dry out without over-browning.

Pratie Oaten

This potato and oat cake is known as 'rozel' in Co. Antrim. Despite the inclusion of potato (a relative newcomer to Ireland as it was only introduced in the sixteenth century), it is not unlike traditional oatcakes, although it is not intended to be dried out like an oatcake. There are no set quantities for the ingredients — it depends on how much leftover cooked potato you have and how much oatmeal these can absorb. Pratie Oaten makes a delicious alternative to potatoes as a vegetable or side dish and deserves to be more widely used in the same way as potato galettes or rösti.

> **cooked potatoes**
> **fine pinhead oatmeal**
> **salt, to taste**

Mash the potatoes and work enough pinhead oatmeal into them to form a dough. Sprinkle the work surface with more oatmeal and roll the dough out fairly thinly. Cut into farls, or use a 2"-3"/5-7 cm round cutter to stamp out circles. Bake on a hot griddle or fry in bacon fat. Best eaten hot with plenty of butter.

Oatmeal Pancakes

These have the flavour of oatmeal but with the runny texture of a pancake batter. Delicious for breakfast with a rasher/slice of bacon tucked inside. Makes about 8.

> **4 oz/100g/1 cup fine wholemeal (whole-wheat) flour**
> **1 oz/25g/2 US tbsp fine pinhead oatmeal**
> **pinch of salt**
> **2 eggs**
> **scant ½ pint/275 ml/1¼ cups (approx.) buttermilk**
> **dripping, to fry**

Mix the flour, oatmeal and salt in a bowl or food processor. Beat in the eggs and enough buttermilk to make a creamy batter, the same consistency as ordinary pancakes. Thoroughly heat a griddle or cast-iron frying pan over quite a high flame. When very hot, grease lightly with dripping. Pour in the pancake batter, about a soup ladle at a time for a large pan. Tilt the pan around to spread evenly. Cook for about 2 minutes on the first side, or until the batter has set and the underside is nicely browned. Flip over and cook for 1 minute on the second side, or until browned. Roll up loosely with a grilled rasher/slice of bacon in each pancake. Serve with grilled sausages (traditional or home-made), eggs and tomato.

Lacken House Potato Cakes

These are similar to Pratie Oaten, except that flour is mixed with cooked potato instead of oatmeal. Eugene McSweeney, chef-owner of Lacken House, Kilkenny, uses the time-honoured method of making them on a griddle or in a heavy frying pan. Traditionally buttered and eaten hot with sugar. Serves 4.

> **1½ lb/700g potatoes**
> **salt, to taste**
> **1 oz/25g/¼ stick unsalted butter**
> **6 oz/175g/1½ cups plain (all-purpose) flour (approx.)**

Peel the potatoes and boil until tender. Drain well, mash and add salt. Mix in the butter and allow to cool a little. Turn out onto a floured work surface and knead in about ⅓ of its volume in flour — enough to make a pliable dough. It will get easier to handle as the flour is incorporated, but *do not over-work it*. Roll out to about ⅓ "/1.5 cm thick and cut into triangles. Heat a dry griddle or heavy frying pan over low heat. Cook for about 3 minutes on each side until browned. Serve hot.

Variation

If you decide to fry this mixture, you are making a northern speciality known as 'fadge', an indispensable part of the great Ulster Fry. Have some hot bacon fat smoking in a heavy frying pan and fry the potato cake in it until brown on both sides. Serve immediately with fried rashers/bacon slices, sausages, eggs and tomatoes for breakfast or high tea.

Apple Fadge

Margaret Erwin, of the Old Bank House in Ballymoney, Co. Antrim, says this was a firm favourite in the home bakery run by her mother-in-law in Ahoghill. It makes a dish like a savoury apple turnover which is baked in the oven and pronounced 'absolutely delicious with pork chops'. Makes 4.

> 1 lb/450g mashed potatoes, preferably still hot
> ½ tsp salt
> 1 oz/25g/¼ stick butter, melted
> 4 oz/100g/1 cup plain (all-purpose) flour (approx.)
> cooked apple

Preheat a fairly hot oven, about 400°F/200°C/gas 6.

Add salt and butter to the mashed potatoes and mix. Knead in enough flour to make a pliable paste — the quantity of flour depends on the variety of potato, as certain varieties will need more than others. *Do not over-work* as too much kneading toughens the mixture. Halve the dough, roll into two circles and quarter each one to make 4 farls. Take a farl and put some cooked apple onto the centre. Place another farl on top and seal the edges. Bake 15-20 minutes, or until crisp and golden brown. Serve hot.

Boxty

This is a speciality of north-west Ireland and falls into three basic groups — boxty bread or cakes ('boxty on the griddle'); boxty pancakes ('boxty on the pan'); and boxty dumplings, which are less well known. There are countless variations of 'boxty on the griddle', which is made in much the same way as potato cake.

> 1 lb/450g raw potatoes
> 1 lb/450g freshly mashed potatoes
> flour
> salt

Peel the raw potatoes and grate them, using the grater attachment on a food processor, if you have one. Turn them onto a clean linen tea/dish towel and wring them out tightly, catching all the liquid in a mixing bowl. Leave until the starch sinks. Then pour off the clear water on top and discard. Add both the grated and the mashed potatoes to the starchy liquid. Mix well. Work in just enough flour to make a pliable dough (as for Potato Cakes, page 20). Knead lightly, roll out into a circle and cut into farls. Bake on a hot griddle, like potato cakes, then butter and serve hot. Leftovers are good the next day — just slice the boxty, fry in bacon fat and serve with rashers/slices of bacon.

Boxty Dumplings

These are made with the same ingredients as boxty, but the dough (currants and raisins can be added) is traditionally formed into balls about the size of a golf ball after kneading. These are flattened and cooked in lightly salted boiling water for 45 minutes, then drained and served with sweet cornflour sauce, like a steamed pudding.

Boxty Pancakes

The quantities given for these deliciously light Boxty Pancakes ('boxty on the pan') are only a starting point, as the recipe is endlessly variable. The milk and flour can be adjusted according to how thin you like your pancakes. Cooked mashed potatoes can be included, but enough milk must always be added to form a dropping consistency. Serves 4.

    1 lb/450g potatoes
    2-3 oz/50-75g/4-6 US tbsp plain (all-purpose) flour
    ¼ pint/150 ml/½ cup milk (approx.)
    salt, to taste

Peel and chop the raw potatoes. Process in a blender or food processor until the potato is thoroughly liquidised. Add flour and enough milk to give a dropping consistency. Season to taste with salt. Heat a little butter or dripping on a griddle or cast-iron frying pan. Pour some of the mixture onto the pan. If the consistency is correct, it will spread evenly over the pan. Cook over moderate heat for about 5 minutes on each side, depending on the thickness of the cake. Serve rolled with a hot filling such as fried chopped bacon and cabbage.

Pancakes with Apple & Ginger Marmalade

Old traditions meet the new in this recipe from Crookedwood House near Mullingar. Owner-chef Noel Kenny serves it as a first course for 4.

    2 lb/900g potatoes
    2 oz/50g/4 US tbsp plain (all-purpose) flour
    grated nutmeg
    salt
    freshly ground pepper
    2 eggs
    ¼ pint/150 ml/½ cup cream
    ¼ pint/150 ml/½ cup milk

Peel the potatoes, then boil them until tender. Drain and mash. Add the flour, a grating of nutmeg and seasoning. Mix well. Add the eggs, one at a time. Then stir in the cream. Finally, add the milk slowly until the mixture reaches dropping consistency. Set aside and leave to rest while making the sauce.

The sauce

zest and juice of 1 orange
2 cooking apples
¼ tsp ground ginger
1 oz/25g/1 US tbsp sugar

Wash the orange. Using a vegetable peeler, remove the zest. Cut it into strips and put into boiling water for a couple of minutes to blanch; drain. Peel, core and chop the apples. Combine all ingredients in a saucepan and cook gently until soft.

Cooking the pancakes

When required, heat a heavy frying pan. Add a little butter or olive oil, then swirl in a ladle of the pancake mixture. Cook until set and nicely browned on both sides. Serve hot with the sauce.

Longueville Potato Cakes

William O'Callaghan, one of Ireland's most talented young chefs, creates sophisticated dinners at Longueville House, Co. Cork and balances them with the utter simplicity of dishes like this. His potato cakes are spicy, thick and firm enough to cut out with a pastry cutter. Delicious served with rashers/slices of bacon and black pudding* for breakfast. Could also be varied and used as a base for mixtures such as fish cakes. Makes about 8-10.

3 oz/75g/¾ stick butter
¼ pint/150 ml/½ cup cream or milk
1 lb/450g mashed potatoes
2 egg yolks
1 onion, diced and lightly sautéed
1 tbsp/1¼ US tbsp parsley, chopped
¼ tsp cumin
grating of nutmeg
salt
black pepper, freshly ground

Melt the butter in a saucepan. Add the cream or milk and heat the two together. Remove from the heat and add the potatoes, then the egg yolks, mixing them in well. Turn the mixture into a large bowl and add the sautéed onion. Add the parsley, cumin, nutmeg and a good seasoning of salt and freshly ground pepper. Mix well. Flour a work surface well and turn the mixture onto it. Then, with a well-floured rolling pin, roll out the mixture to a thickness of 1"/2.5 cm. Cut out the cakes with a pastry cutter. To cook, heat a heavy pan or griddle thoroughly, add some butter and lightly fry the potato cakes in it until they are golden-brown on both sides.

'Black pudding' and 'white pudding' are sausage products similar to German wursts. They are less fatty as they contain more grain or meal.

Buttermilk Griddle Scones

These are similar to the more common 'drop scones', except that buttermilk and bread/baking soda are used instead of baking powder and sweet milk. A little golden/Karo syrup is sometimes used instead of the caster/superfine sugar. If mixing by hand, blend it in with the egg and buttermilk before beating. Makes about 12.

> 4 oz/100g/1 cup plain (all-purpose) flour
> pinch of salt
> 1 tsp/1¼ US tsp bread (baking) soda
> 1 oz/25g/1 US tbsp caster (superfine) sugar
> 1 egg
> ¼ pint/150 ml/½ cup buttermilk

Put all ingredients into a blender or food processor and blend until smooth. Pour the batter into a jug or bowl and set beside the hob. Heat a griddle or a heavy frying pan over moderate heat. When well heated, rub over lightly with a little white fat. Place tablespoons of the batter onto the griddle, spaced well apart. Cook until bubbles rise to the surface. Then loosen with a spatula and flip over and cook for a minute or so on the second side. Remove from the pan and keep warm in a basket lined with a tea/dish towel or napkin. Lightly grease the pan again between batches. Serve warm with butter and jam.

Hilton Park Pancakes with Apples & Honey

In rolling parkland on the Monaghan border near Lough Erne stands stately Hilton Park. It has been in the Madden family since the mid-eighteenth century and is magnificently maintained. Along with a carefully judged balance between luxury and informality, the beautiful grounds and Lucy Madden's renowned cooking share equal claims to fame. Much of the food served to guests comes from the estate — there's a biodynamic garden as well as farmland and lakes. Although dinner overlooking the parkland in the fading light is memorable, the meal which guests recall most vividly is breakfast, taken in the sun-filled green breakfast room, where delights such as these pancakes are served. Makes 18 small panakes.

Pancakes
4 oz/100g/1 cup self-raising flour
pinch of salt
1 large egg, separated
¾ pint/450 ml/1⅔ cups buttermilk
oil, for frying

Filling
2 large cooking apples, peeled and sliced
knob of butter
2 fl oz/50 ml/2 US tbsp honey
pinch of cinnamon (optional)
grated lemon zest

First make the pancake batter. Sift the flour and salt together. Separate the egg and beat the yolk into the buttermilk. Stir gradually into the flour and beat well until the mixture is smooth. Beat the egg white until stiff, then fold into the mixture.

To cook, heat a griddle, oil lightly and cook the pancakes by spooning out into 4"/10 cm rounds. Cook until both sides are golden.

Meanwhile, prepare the filling. Peel and slice the apples. Melt the butter and honey and cook the apples in it until they are just soft. Add the cinnamon, if using, and the lemon zest.

When the pancakes are cooked, lay them out on warmed serving plates and divide the apple mixture between them. Then fold the pancakes over and pour a little of the left-over buttery honey juices over each one. Eat at once.

Flower Crêpes with Summer Berry Filling

At the Old Rectory on the edge of Wicklow town, Linda Saunders enjoys a remarkable reputation for her unique floral cuisine. This modern recipe is typical of her style. Edible flowers which are suitable for decorating crêpes include violets, violas, primroses and polyanthus, rose petals, carnation petals and marigolds. Dark petals work best against these bright yellow crêpes, making a dramatic and unusual dessert. Makes 10 crêpes.

Crêpes
4 oz/100g/1 cup plain (all-purpose) flour
½ tsp salt
1 tbsp/1¼ US tbsp caster (superfine) sugar
½ pint/300 ml/1¼ cups milk
2 large free-range eggs (preferably duck eggs)
flower petals

Filling
9 fl oz/250 ml/scant 1¼ cups cream
6 punnets (US pint containers) mixed summer berries
extra caster (superfine) sugar

Prepare the crêpes. Sift dry ingredients into a bowl and beat in the liquids until smooth. Let the mixture stand for at least 3 hours before cooking.

To cook the crêpes
Heat a pancake pan and wipe with a little oil on a tissue before each pancake is cooked. Pour a little batter into the pan and swirl it around to make a thin disc. While the mixture is still runny, press the prepared flower petals and heads into the surface, face up. Turn the pancake and cook lightly on the other side. Interleave the pancakes with pieces of baking parchment/waxed paper on a plate until you want them.

To assemble
Whip the cream until stiff. Prepare the soft fruit according to type. Lay the pancakes, flower side down, on serving plates. Put a band of cream across each, then the berries. Sprinkle with sugar. Roll up and arrange so that the flowers are on top. Surround the pancakes with a fairly sharp fruit purée, made by liquidising any spare or imperfect fruit with a little lemon juice and sugar to taste. Garnish with a few fresh berries and fresh or frosted flowers.

To make frosted flowers

Take 1 egg white and stir in a little water until it is just broken up and slightly frothy. Using a small brush, paint the surface of each flower or petal (being careful not to leave gaps, as flowers will go off quickly). Then dust evenly with caster (superfine) sugar. Leave on a wire tray in an airy place to dry. Many flowers are suitable for this, but as a useful rule of thumb, avoid the flowers of bulbs, many of which are inedible.

Hunter's Drop Scones

Hunter's Hotel outside Wicklow town is one of Ireland's oldest coaching inns, now in its fifth generation of family ownership. It was already receiving honourable mention from travellers in the eighteenth century, when diaries were *de rigeur* and provided the earliest form of guide book. Whether at the fireside on a crisp winter's day or beside their renowned riverside herbaceous border in summer, afternoon tea is the high point of the day at Hunter's, where a selection of traditional treats is served, including these drop scones. Makes about 24.

> 8 oz/225g/2 cups plain (all-purpose) flour
> ½ level tsp bread (baking) soda
> 1 level tsp/1¼ US tsp baking powder
> 1 tbsp/1¼ US tbsp sugar
> ½ tsp salt
> lemon rind, finely grated
> 1 egg
> ½ pint/300 ml/1¼ cups milk (approx.)

Sift together the flour, soda and baking powder. Mix in the sugar, salt and lemon rind and make a hollow in the middle. Add the egg and beat in with enough milk to make a stiff batter. Allow to stand for 15 minutes.

Meanwhile, heat a griddle or heavy frying pan thoroughly and grease with a little oil or white fat. Ladle spoonsful of the batter at intervals around the griddle. Cook for 2 or 3 minutes, until bubbles rise to the top. Then flip over and cook for the same time so that the scones are nicely browned on both sides.

Hot Drop Pancakes

Afternoon tea is a speciality at Currarevagh, the Hodgson family's delightful country house in Oughterard, Connemara. Famous for its fishing, anglers return to the garden or elegant drawing room and are treated to delicious home-baking for afternoon tea. June Hodgson's unusual pancakes have whisked egg white folded in, producing a lovely light, fluffy texture. Makes 30 tiny pancakes.

> 2 tbsp/2½ US tbsp plain (all-purpose) flour
> 1 tbsp/1¼ US tbsp sugar
> 1 level tsp/1¼ US tsp baking powder
> 1 level tsp/1¼ US tsp bread (baking) soda
> 1 egg, separated
> a little milk
> lard/white fat, for frying
> caster (superfine) sugar, for sprinkling

Combine the flour, sugar, baking powder and soda and mix well. Separate the egg. Make a well in the dry ingredients and drop in the yolk. Beat with a little milk until there are no lumps. Whip the white of egg until a firm foam is formed, then fold it carefully into the flour and egg mixture with a metal spoon.

Cook the pancakes in batches. Heat a little lard or white fat in a heavy frying pan. When it is very hot, drop small dessertspoons of the mixture onto the pan and quickly flip over to brown both sides evenly. Transfer to a plate lined with kitchen paper to dry out. As soon as they are all ready, serve immediately, sprinkled with caster (superfine) sugar.

Griddle-baked Soda Farls

These are delicious served fresh with plenty of butter. But they will keep longer than oven-baked bread and come into their own after a day or two when they're split and toasted or, better still, fried in bacon fat and with an egg on top to provide an essential ingredient of that great high tea speciality, the Ulster Fry. Curiously enough, there's hardly a soda farl to be found south of the River Boyne, although they're in every baker's window in the north.

This excellent recipe is adapted from the one used at Arthur McCann Ltd, the renowned Victoria Bakery in Newry. If you don't have a griddle, use a heavy cast-iron frying pan, but be careful not to make the farls too thick or you'll end up with a thick crust and the dough still uncooked in the centre — ½ "/1.2 cm is deep enough. Use two pans, or make a smaller quantity so they're not too thick and cook more evenly.

In the north of Ireland they use 'soda flour', with the soda included. When it is unavailable, self-raising flour can be used instead, or you can add your own soda.

Griddle baking is a skill like making pancakes, so don't be discouraged if you have to put your first attempt down to experience. If the pan is too hot, you will find that the outside burns before the centre is cooked, so cook more gently the next time. If the dough is too slack, reduce the buttermilk in future. Makes 4-8 farls.

> 1 lb/450g/4 cups flour
> 1 tsp/1¼ US tsp bread (baking) soda
> good pinch of salt
> 1 tsp vegetable oil (optional)
> 16 fl oz/450 ml/2 cups buttermilk (approx.)

Sift the dry ingredients in a bowl. Add oil and buttermilk. Mix as quickly and lightly as possible with the hands or a wooden spoon to make a soft dough. Turn onto a floured surface. Dredge the dough with flour and knead lightly by turning the corners into the centre, turning the whole round as you do so. Have a griddle or a large heavy frying pan heating on the hob. Roll out the dough lightly to make a circle not more than ½ "/1.2 cm thick. Cut a deep cross in it to make four farls. Test that the pan is ready by sprinkling a little flour on it — it should brown quickly. Lift the farls onto the hot griddle and cook for 6-7 minutes, then turn and cook for the same time on the second side. To test if the farls are cooked, open up at the edge. When ready, the dough will be dry inside. Cool on a wire rack.

Clonbrook Breakfast Scones

Tullanisk, the Dower House of Birr Castle in Co. Offaly, is set in woodland gardens which harbour a plethora of wildlife. The house, run by George and Susie Gossip, has great charm and George's skills in the kitchen are renowned. Lucky guests wake to the dawn chorus and the aroma of their scones which, says George, were obtained by Robert, 3rd Lord Clonbrook, when staying on the Aran Islands around 1850. Makes 8.

> ½ lb/225g/2 cups wholemeal (whole-wheat) flour
> salt, to taste
> 2 oz/50g/½ stick margarine or butter
> buttermilk

Blend flour and salt in a mixing bowl. Rub in the margarine. Mix in enough buttermilk to make a rather soft dough. Roll out to a rectangle about ½"/1.2 cm thick. Mark out and cut to make 8 squares — if you try to make more, they will be too thin. To cook, grease a griddle or heavy frying pan lightly with buttered paper, then heat slowly. Lay the scones on the hot surface and cook gently, flipping over when the under-side is brown. When ready, the scones should be brown on the outside but soft and almost raw in the middle.

Roundwood House Griddle Scones

At the Kennans' enchanting small Palladian villa, Roundwood House, Co. Laois, Rosemarie Kennan serves these scones for breakfast straight from the Aga. She cooks them on an old cast-iron griddle and finds the even temperature on the Aga hot plate much better than modern gas or electric hobs for this old family recipe. Makes 8.

> 5 oz/150g/scant 1¼ cups wholemeal (whole-wheat) flour
> l oz/25g/1 US tbsp oat flakes
> l flat tsp bread (baking) soda
> salt
> 7 fl oz/200 ml/⅔ cup buttermilk (approx.)

Have a griddle or heavy frying pan heating on the hob. Mix the dry ingredients well in a bowl. Stir in enough buttermilk to make a *very wet consistency*. Lightly grease the griddle, or sprinkle it with flour. Put dessertspoonsful of the mixture onto the hot griddle and cook for 5-6 minutes on each side, until well risen and golden-brown. Wrap in a clean tea/dish towel and serve hot or cold, with butter and home-made jam.

Tea Breads, Bracks & Buns

Tea breads, bracks and buns are the kinds of comforting, everyday baked goods that were once part of every Irish family's normal baking pattern. Although not yet a thing of the past, it is now less common for people to take the time to make them than it was a generation ago.

The positive side of this story of decline is a new appreciation of those good things which so many people remember from childhood, coupled with a determination not to let the skills, or the quality of home life associated with them, slip away entirely. These simple tea breads, bracks and buns still have a special place on the afternoon tea tray and the high tea tables which are an integral part of holidays on farms and at country guesthouses.

Tea bread could be defined as a light cake, halfway between a bread and a cake. Often served sliced and buttered like scones, it is part of a baking category which includes all sorts of simple, everyday things — including the brack itself. This is probably the most Irish of all cakes and gets it name from the word *breac*, meaning 'speckled'. There are two basic types of brack — one made with yeast and known as Barm Brack, and the other made with baking powder and called Tea Brack because the dried fruit is soaked in cold tea before mixing.

Barm Brack (page 110) is now mainly a Hallowe'en speciality. However, it has been associated with a variety of other festivals, notably St Brigid's Day celebrated on 1 February (traditionally the first day of spring in Ireland) and the festival of Lughnasa, which began the harvest on 1 August (traditionally the first day of autumn). Tea bracks, which are simpler to make, are more likely to be made throughout the year like other cakes.

Fruit Soda Bread

Although it is made almost everywhere in Ireland, this is the quintessential tea bread of Northern Ireland. A fruited version of plain white soda, it is sure to be among the many delicious bakes on the farmhouse tea table. In her book *Irish Traditional Cooking*, Darina Allen says they have always called this 'Spotted Dog'. It is known as 'currnie' or 'railway cake' in different parts of the country. Makes 1 'cake' or 4 farls.

1 lb/450g/4 cups plain (all-purpose) flour
1 level tsp salt
l level tsp/1¼ US tsp bread (baking) soda
2 tbsp/2½ US tbsp sugar
2 oz/50g/½ stick butter (optional)
4 oz/100g/¾ cup currants or raisins
1 oz/25g/¼ cup cut mixed peel
1 egg, beaten (optional)
8 fl oz/225 ml/1 cup buttermilk (approx.)

Preheat a hot oven, 425°F/220°C/gas 7.

Sift the flour, salt and soda into a mixing bowl. Add sugar. Rub in the butter, if using. Add the cleaned fruit. Mix quickly and lightly with the beaten egg, if using, and enough buttermilk to make a fairly soft dough. Turn the mixture onto a floured board, dredge the dough with flour and knead it lightly. When smooth underneath, turn it upside down and roll out lightly to make a round. Cut a deep cross in the middle to make 4 farls. Put on a floured baking sheet and bake for 45 minutes, until risen, nicely brown and cooked to the centre. It should sound hollow when the base is tapped. Cool on a wire rack. Use on the day of baking, or the next day, toasted and served hot with butter.

Tea Brack

An unyeasted version of the traditional Barm Brack (page 110), this is more widely made than the original. It is particularly popular at Hallowe'en, when a ring or other symbolic charms may be added (see 'Festive Fare'). Makes 1 x 9"/23cm brack.

8 oz/225g/1⅓ cups raisins
8 oz/225g/1⅓ cups sultanas (dried green grapes)
6 oz/175g/⅔ cup dark soft brown sugar
½ pint/300 ml/1¼ cups cold, strong tea
4 oz/100g/¾ cup mixed peel
grated rind of 1 (washed) orange
4 oz/100g/1 stick butter, melted
2 eggs, lightly beaten
l lb/450g/4 cups plain (all-purpose) flour
2 level tsp/2½ US tsp baking powder
l tsp mixed spice
½ tsp cinnamon
pinch of salt
ring wrapped in grease-proof/waxed paper (optional)

Put the raisins, sultanas and brown sugar in a saucepan with the strained tea. Bring slowly up to boiling point, stirring occasionally. Allow to cool. It can be left overnight, if convenient.

Preheat a moderate oven, 350°F/180°C/gas 4. Grease and base-line a 9"/22 cm round deep cake tin.

Add the mixed peel and grated orange rind to the mixture, along with the melted butter and lightly beaten eggs. Sift the dry ingredients together and gradually stir into the fruit mixture. Stir well, making sure all ingredients are thoroughly mixed together. Add the ring, if using. Turn the mixture into the prepared tin and bake for 1½ -2 hours, until the top of the cake feels firm to the touch. Remove from the oven and brush with a glaze made by bringing 2 tbsp of water to the boil in a small pan and dissolving 1 tbsp of sugar in it. Return the brack to the oven for about 3 minutes, until the top is shiny brown. Cool in the tin and serve sliced and buttered.

Variations

*Whiskey Brack
Up to ¼ pint/150 ml/½ cup Irish whiskey can be used to replace some of the tea, if preferred.

*Cider Brack
Using cider instead of tea produces a brack which is lighter but especially juicy and flavoursome. Very good toasted and spread with cinnamon butter.

*Porter Cake
If the tea is replaced by stout (Guinness, Beamish or Murphy's), you will have a simple, lighter version of the traditional Irish Porter Cake.

Irish Tea Cake

This cake is made regularly by Lindy O'Hara for her guests at Coopershill in Co. Sligo, one of the loveliest of Ireland's country houses. It is a cross between a brack and a fruit cake, as it contains chopped nuts and glacé cherries — traditional in fruit cakes but not in bracks. It makes a dark, moist tea bread that keeps well. Makes 2 small loaves.

> 1 lb/450g/2½ cups mixed dried fruits (sultanas, raisins,
>   currants, mixed peel etc.)
> ½ pint/300 ml/1¼ cups strong cold tea
> 8 oz/225g/1 cup demerara (granulated brown) sugar
> 4 oz/100g/⅔ cup chopped walnuts
> 4 oz/100g/⅔ cup glacé cherries, rinsed, dried and quartered
> 1 large egg, beaten together with 2 tbsp milk
> 1 lb/450g/4 cups self-raising flour

Prepare the fruit by soaking it in the cold tea with the sugar overnight.

Next day, preheat a very moderate oven, 325°F/170°C/gas 3 and grease two 1 lb/450g loaf tins thoroughly.

Stir the remaining ingredients into the soaked fruit. Turn the mixture into the prepared tins. Bake in the centre of the oven for about 1 hour and 10 minutes, until golden-brown on top and springy to the touch in the centre. Then turn the loaves onto a wire rack, right side up. As soon as the loaves are cool, they can be cut into slices about ½"/1.2 cm thick and served thickly spread with butter.

Buttermilk Cake

This light fruit cake is usually eaten sliced and buttered, like a tea bread. Unlike the previous recipes, it is a rubbed-in mixture and the fruit is included with the dry ingredients. Makes 1 cake.

> 12 oz/350g/3 cups plain (all-purpose) flour
> 4 oz/100g/1 stick butter
> 4 oz/100g/½ cup soft dark brown sugar
> 3 oz/75g/½ cup raisins
> 3 oz/75g/½ cup currants
> good pinch of mixed spice
> 1 rounded tsp/1¼ US tsp baking powder
> l egg, lightly beaten
> about ½ pint/300 ml/1¼ cups buttermilk

Preheat a moderate oven, 350°F/180°C/gas 4. Grease and base-line a 7"-8"/18-20 cm deep cake tin.

Sift the flour and rub in the butter until the mixture looks like fine breadcrumbs. Add all the remaining dry ingredients and mix well. Beat the egg lightly and add it with enough buttermilk to make a dropping consistency. Turn the mixture into the prepared tin and bake for about 1½ hours, until the top is springy to the touch and a skewer pushed into the centre of the cake comes out clean. Turn out and cool on a rack.

Date Cake

This simple cake is typical of the rubbed-in recipes which have always been popular in farmhouse kitchens. They are quick to prepare and inexpensive but, unlike richer creamed mixtures which keep longer, they are generally best when eaten fresh. The dates in this recipe keep it moist for longer than most, however. It is good toasted and buttered like a brack. Makes 1 cake.

> 8 oz/225g/2 cups self-raising flour
> pinch of salt
> pinch of mixed spice
> 4 oz/100g/1 stick butter
> 4 oz/100g/½ cup granulated sugar
> 4 oz/100g/⅔ cup pressed dates, chopped
> 1 egg, beaten
> a little milk, to mix
> 1 tbsp/1¼ US tbsp granulated sugar, to sprinkle

Preheat a moderate oven, 350°F/180°C/gas 4. Grease and base-line a 7-8"/18-20 cm deep cake tin, preferably loose-based.

Sift together the flour, salt and spice. Rub in the butter. Add the sugar and the chopped dates (stones removed). Mix in the beaten egg and enough milk to make a dropping consistency. Turn into the prepared tin. Sprinkle a tablespoon of sugar over the top to make a crunchy crust. Bake for 1½ hours, until golden-brown and firm to the touch. Allow to cool a little in the tin, then turn out onto a wire rack. Store in an airtight tin when cold.

Variation

*Light Cherry Cake
The same recipe can be used to make a Light Cherry Cake. Omit the spice and add a little grated lemon peel, if you like. Replace the dates with chopped glacé cherries. See also Chapter 6.

Traditional Gingerbread

Along with almonds and caraway seeds, ground ginger is one of the most traditional of ingredients in Irish baking, having been popular since the eighteenth century. Coincidentally, perhaps, both ginger and caraway are reputed to aid the digestion.

Careful baking of this gingerbread is important to prevent burning because of the amount of treacle or syrup used. This recipe makes a dense, slightly sticky cake with a rich but not aggressive gingery flavour. A fairly shallow baking tin — not more than about 2"/5 cm deep — with straight sides will make it easier to cut the gingerbread into fingers or squares.

> 1 lb/450g/4 cups flour
> ½ tsp salt
> 1½ - 2 tsp ground ginger (or more, to taste)
> 2 tsp/2½ US tsp baking powder
> ½ tsp bread (baking) soda
> 8 oz/225g/1 cup demerara (granulated brown) sugar
> 6 oz/175g/1½ sticks butter or margarine
> 12 oz/350g/1⅓ cups treacle (molasses) or syrup (Karo) or a mixture
> ½ pint/300 ml/1¼ cups milk
> 1 large egg, beaten

Preheat a moderate oven, 350°F/180°C/gas 4. Grease and base-line a tin 9"/23 cm square or an oblong, about 10"x 8"/26 x 20 cm.

Sift all the dry ingredients *except the sugar* together. Warm the sugar, fat and treacle/syrup gently in a pan over low heat until the fat has just melted. *Do not overheat*. Make a well in the dry ingredients and stir in the melted syrup mixture, along with the milk and beaten egg. Mix very thoroughly. Pour the mixture into the prepared tin and bake for about 1½ hours, until well-risen and just firm to the touch. Cool in the tin for 15 minutes, then turn out onto a wire rack and leave until cold.

To store, leave the lining paper in place and wrap the gingerbread in greaseproof/waxed paper and foil. Leave for a few days, preferably a week, allowing the flavours to mellow before cutting into fingers or chunks.

Hunter's Ginger Cake

This makes a regular appearance at afternoon tea in the garden or by the fireside at Hunter's Hotel in Rathnew, Co. Wicklow. Simpler than the traditional gingerbread given above, it's a quick all-in-one cake baked in a loaf tin like a tea bread for easy slicing. Makes 1 large loaf.

> 8 oz/225g/2 cups flour
> 4 oz/100g/1 stick butter or block margarine, at room temperature
> 2 tbsp/2½ US tbsp golden (Karo) syrup
> 1 egg
> 2 tsp ground ginger
> 1 tsp/1¼ US tsp bread (baking) soda
> ¼ pint/150 ml/½ cup milk

Preheat a moderate oven, 350°F/180°C/gas 4. Grease a 2 lb/900g loaf tin. Put all ingredients into a mixing bowl and mix everything together until smooth. Turn into the prepared tin and bake in the centre of the oven for 1 hour, until springy to the touch and shrinking slightly from the tin. Turn out and cool on a wire rack. Wrap and store in an airtight tin for a few days before cutting.

Oatmeal Gingerbread

Similar to Ginger Parkin, this bread is dark and moist, with a nuttier texture and slightly milder flavour than traditional gingerbread. Makes 1 loaf.

> 6 oz/175g/1½ cups plain (all-purpose) flour
> 2 oz/50g/½ stick butter
> 2 oz/50g/4 US tbsp fine oatmeal
> 2 oz/50g/¼ cup dark soft brown sugar
> 1 tsp ground ginger
> ¾ tsp bread (baking) soda
> 1 tbsp/1¼ US tbsp each of treacle (molasses) and
>   golden (Karo) syrup (or 2 tbsp treacle/molasses)
> 1 egg, beaten
> buttermilk, as required (see below)

Preheat a moderate oven, 350°F/180°C/gas 4. Generously grease a shallow baking tin, 7½ -8"/19-20 cm square, or an oblong one about 9"x 6½ "/23 x 16 cm.

Measure the flour into a mixing bowl. Rub in the butter. Then mix in all the other dry ingredients. Warm the treacle/syrup and mix in. Add the beaten egg and enough buttermilk to make a soft dropping consistency. Pour into the prepared tin and bake for about 1 hour, until well-risen and firm in the centre. Cool slightly in the tin, then turn out onto a wire rack. Wrap and store in an airtight tin for a few days before use.

Variation

If buttermilk is unavailable, add ½ tsp sifted cream of tartar to the dry ingredients. Or use 1 heaped tsp of baking powder to replace the bread soda, and use sweet milk instead.

Gingerbread Buns

That great traditional ingredient — the almond — makes an appearance in these easy little buns. The blanched almond in the base of each bun makes a nice crunchy surprise. Makes 10-12.

> 4 oz/100g/1 cup plain (all-purpose) flour
> scant ½ tsp bread (baking) soda
> 1 oz/25g/¼ stick butter
> scant 1 oz/25g/1 US tbsp sugar
> ½ tsp ground ginger
> pinch of mixed spice
> 1 good tbsp treacle (molasses) or syrup (Karo), melted
> 1 small egg, beaten
> a little milk, if required
> blanched almonds, halved

Preheat a moderate oven, 350°F/180°C/gas 4. Thoroughly grease 10-12 bun/ cupcake tins and place half an almond in the bottom of each one. Sift the flour and soda together. Rub in the butter, then add the sugar and spices. Mix well. Blend in the melted treacle/syrup, the beaten egg and, if required, enough milk to make a soft consistency. Spoon into the prepared bun tins, not more than half-full. Bake for about 20 minutes, until well-risen and firm to the touch.

Cherry & Almond Buns

Due to their unique properties — subtle flavour, moistness and varied textures — almonds have been popular since the eighteenth century and have never gone out of fashion. Add them to glacé cherries (which taste delicious and retain moisture beautifully, keeping baked goods fresh much longer than usual), and you have a winning combination. Although prepared almonds — blanched halves, flakes, nibbed (chopped) almonds etc. — are convenient, blanching them yourself and preparing them freshly will make a big difference to any recipe; they will have better flavour and more moisture. Makes about 12.

> 3 oz/75g/½ cup plain (all-purpose) flour
> 1 oz/25g/2 US tbsp cornflour (corn starch)
> ½ tsp baking powder
> 1 oz/25g/¼ cup almonds, blanched and chopped
> 2 oz/50g/½ cup glacé cherries, chopped
> 4 oz/100g/1 stick butter or margarine
> 4 oz/100g/½ cup caster (superfine) sugar
> 2 eggs
> a little milk, if required

Preheat a moderately hot oven, 375°F/190°C/gas 5. Grease about 12 deep bun/ cupcake tins.

Sift the flour, cornflour/corn starch and baking powder together. Mix in the chopped almonds and cherries. Cream the butter and sugar until light and fluffy, then gradually beat in the eggs. Fold lightly into the flour mixture, adding a little milk, if necessary, to make a soft dropping consistency. Place in spoonsful in the greased tins, not more than half-filling them. Bake for about 20 minutes, until well-risen, golden-brown and springy to the touch. Cool on a wire rack. When cold, they can be decorated with glacé icing and glacé cherries.

Raspberry Buns

These crunchy little treats are delicious made with home-made raspberry jam and eaten warm from the oven. Makes 12 buns.

> 8 oz/225g/2 cups plain (all-purpose) flour
> 1½ tsp/1¾ US tsp baking powder
> pinch of salt
> 3 oz/75g/¾ stick butter
> 4 oz/100g/½ cup caster (superfine) sugar
> 1 large egg, beaten
> a little milk to mix
> home-made raspberry jam
> granulated sugar (optional)

Preheat a very hot oven, 450°F/230°C/gas 8.

Sift the flour, baking powder and salt into a mixing bowl. Rub in the butter and add the sugar. Beat the egg lightly and add to the dry ingredients with enough milk to make a fairly stiff dough.

Turn onto a floured work surface and divide into 12 equal portions. Using a little flour to prevent sticking, roll the dough into balls and lay them, spaced well apart, on a greased baking tray (or in greased bun/cupcake tins). Using a teaspoon, make a hole in the middle of each ball and fill it with raspberry jam. Then pinch together to close the dough over again. Flatten the balls slightly with the back of a spoon or fork, brush with a little milk and sprinkle with the granulated sugar to make a crunchy topping. Bake for 15-20 minutes, until golden-brown and firm to the touch. When ready, the buns should crack on top to reveal the jam inside.

Cashel House Banana Bread

Bananas make very moist cakes and tea breads that keep well. This unusual bread has long been a favourite at Cashel House, Connemara, where it is popular as a delicious tea bread or toasted and served with cream and home-made strawberry jam. The sunflower seeds give it a contrasting crunchy texture, while the marmalade adds a tangy snap to the flavour. Makes 2 loaves.

> 1 lb/450g/4 cups self-raising flour
> 2 oz/50g/½ stick butter
> 4 oz/100g/½ cup caster (superfine) sugar
> 2 oz/50g/¼ cup sunflower seeds, toasted
> 4 ripe bananas, mashed
> 2 tbsp/2 ½ US tbsp marmalade
> 4 eggs
> few drops natural vanilla essence

Preheat a moderate oven, 350°F/180°C/gas 4. Grease and base-line two 2 lb/900g loaf tins.

Sift the flour into a mixing bowl. Cut in the butter and rub in to make a mixture like fine breadcrumbs. Mix in the sugar and sunflower seeds. Mash the bananas to a purée and blend with the marmalade. Crack the eggs into a bowl and lightly whisk in the vanilla essence. Add the banana mixture to the flour, followed by the eggs. Mix everything together thoroughly. Divide between the two loaf tins and put into the preheated oven, immediately reducing the temperature to very moderate, 300°F/150°C/gas 2. Bake for 40 minutes, until golden-brown, springy to the touch and shrinking slightly from the sides of the tins. Cool in the tins for a few minutes, then turn out onto wire racks. When cold, store in an airtight tin.

American Banana Bread

Blairs Cove, the atmospheric waterside restaurant in West Cork, is renowned for its buffet displays of hors d'oeuvres and desserts. Amidst all the rich puddings, simpler alternatives such as this banana bread can be found. Makes 1 large or 2 small loaves.

> finely grated zest of 1 (washed) lemon
> 4 oz/100g/⅔ cup sultanas (dried green grapes)
> 1 tbsp/1¼ US tbsp rum
> 4 oz/100g/1 stick butter, softened
> 6 oz/175g/¾ cup caster (superfine) sugar
> 2 eggs, beaten
> 14 oz/400g/1¾ cups mashed bananas
> 1 tbsp/1¼ US tbsp lemon juice
> 5 oz/150g/1 cup walnuts, roughly broken
> 11 oz/300g/2¾ cups plain (all-purpose) flour
> 2½ tsp/3 US tsp baking powder
> a little milk, if necessary

Soak the lemon zest, sultanas and rum together until the liquid has been absorbed. Preheat a moderate oven, 350°F/180°C/gas 4. Butter and base-line a large loaf tin (at least 9x5x3"/23x13x7.5) or two smaller ones.

Beat butter and sugar until pale and creamy. Add the beaten eggs, then mix in the soaked fruit. Add the mashed bananas, lemon juice and walnuts. Sift the flour and baking powder together and fold into the mixture lightly but thoroughly, adding a little milk if the mixture seems too stiff. Bake for about 1¼ hours, until golden-brown and springy to the touch. Cool on a wire rack. Store in an airtight tin when cold. Serve sliced, with or without butter.

Variation

Make a Date Loaf by replacing the mashed bananas with the same weight of soaked chopped dates.

Whole-wheat Banana Bread

This is made regularly by Rosemarie Kennan at the eighteenth-century Roundwood House in Co. Laois. Although just as delicious as the previous recipes, it is completely different. The bananas and honey make it moist, but the texture comes from the wholemeal flour, with the traditional bread/baking soda and buttermilk combination as the raising agents. The shape is also quite different — rather than making it as a loaf, Rosemarie bakes it in a Swiss roll/jelly roll tin. Makes 1 cake.

> 8 oz/225g/2 sticks butter or margarine
> 6 tbsp/8 US tbsp honey
> 12 oz/350g/3 cups wholemeal (whole-wheat) flour
> 3 tsp/3¾ US tsp bread soda
> ½ tsp salt
> 4 bananas, mashed
> 4 fl oz/100 ml/scant ½ cup buttermilk, or as required

Grease a Swiss roll/jelly roll tin and preheat a moderate oven, 350°F/180°C/gas 4.
    Cream the butter or margarine and honey until light. Add the dry ingredients and mashed bananas and beat until smooth. Add enough buttermilk to make a wet dough. Stir well. Turn into the prepared tin and bake for 50-60 minutes, until browned, well-risen and springy to the touch. Turn out onto a wire rack and cool before serving.

Yogurt Loaf

Up in Co. Antrim near the Giant's Causeway, Elizabeth Hegarty heartily spoils her guests at the family farm, Greenhill House. On arrival, afternoon tea is served in the drawing room — and with it, as fine a selection of home baking as anyone could wish for, including this loaf. She says she can 'just whip it up without thinking'. The yogurt carton is the only vital piece of equipment for measuring, which makes preparation very quick. Makes 2 small loaves.

> 1 carton hazelnut yogurt
> 1 carton vegetable oil
> 2 cartons granulated sugar
> 3 cartons self-raising flour
> 3 eggs

Preheat a moderate oven, 350°F/180°C/gas 4. Grease and line two 1 lb/450g loaf tins.
    Pour the yogurt, oil and sugar into a bowl and beat for a short time to blend. Add the flour and eggs and beat for a minute or until thoroughly mixed. Pour into the prepared tins and bake for about 30 minutes, until golden-brown and springy to the touch. Turn out and cool on a wire rack. Serve sliced and buttered for tea.

Date & Walnut Loaf

This is another of Elizabeth Hegarty's recipes. It's easy to see the practical mind of a busy woman at work here in the quick and easy melting method.

8 oz/225g/1½ cups dates
4 oz/100g/½ cup caster (superfine) sugar
1 level tsp bread (baking) soda
2 oz/50g/½ stick margarine
6 fl oz/175 ml/¾ cup boiling water
1 egg, beaten
2 oz/50g/½ cup walnuts
8 oz/225g/2 cups self-raising flour
1 tsp/1¼ US tsp vanilla essence

Grease and line two 1 lb/450g loaf tins and preheat a very moderate oven, 300°F/150°C/gas 2.

Place dates, sugar, soda and margarine in a saucepan. Add the boiling water and mix well to melt the margarine. Allow to cool. Then add the beaten egg, walnuts, flour and vanilla essence. Mix well and pour into the prepared tins and bake for 40-50 minutes, until well-risen and springy to the touch. Turn out and cool on a wire rack. Serve sliced and buttered.

Yeast Breads

Home baking with yeast was uncommon in Ireland until recently. With the exception of the white 'priest's loaf', bought from a bakery in honour of a pastoral visit, brown soda bread was the bread of the country. This was due to the tradition of baking on an open hearth, which was not well suited to the demands of baking with yeast.

Yeast cookery also had a reputation for being 'difficult'. So even as kitchens improved and gas and electric ovens made it a practical proposition, unfamiliarity with yeast baking made even the most accomplished home bakers nervous of experiment.

Two relatively recent events have changed this situation, however. The first was the advent of 'easy-mix' or 'fast-action' dried yeast, which brought yeast cookery much closer to the style of the old soda bread tradition. The second was the growing fashion for yeast breads — particularly Mediterranean styles (see 'Speciality Breads'). With coverage in magazines and on television programmes, the spin-off was more interest in home baking with yeast.

Successful yeast cookery requires 'strong' flour with a high gluten content which is developed by kneading to produce the elasticity that enables it to rise properly. Although the familiar 'plain' or 'cream' white wheat flour can be used, Ireland's damp climate produces a softer wheat with a lower gluten content; other traditional grains that work well in soda breads — especially oats — are unsuitable.

With increased consumer demand, 'strong' bakers' flour is now widely available. And, encouraged by their success with fast-action dried yeast, home bakers have begun to use fresh yeast. Because fresh yeast freezes well, it's worth getting a large batch from a specialist supplier and freezing it in 1-2 oz/25-50g packs.

When fresh yeast is unavailable, fast-action dried yeast can be used quite satisfactorily for domestic purposes. For ordinary breads, allow 1 sachet per 1 lb/450g flour (more if fruit or nuts are in the mixture). Otherwise, follow instructions on the pack. The results will not be quite as moist, nor will the loaf keep as well, but it is extremely easy to use.

Included in this section are some true yeast recipes — those which use fresh yeast without any short cuts and which require fermentation, knocking back and rising (proving). Some are marginally different, since they may not contain the small amount of fat normally used to improve the texture of the dough. Some might be described as 'easy traditional', using shortcuts such as easy-blend/fast-action yeast, although they are still kneaded. Others are hybrids of the soda- and yeast-baking traditions, since yeast is used, without kneading to develop the gluten, producing a texture more like soda bread. For easy reference, the recipes are organised in groups which show examples of

   *those which are more or less true to the old yeast baking methods
   *the traditional kneaded mixtures, with some variations
   *hybrids of the yeast- and soda-baking traditions
   *the 'super-hybrids', for which the methods may be 'true' but ingredients

   hybrid. (Other yeast recipes may be found in 'Festive Fare' and 'Speciality Breads'.)
No special equipment is needed for yeast baking — in fact, hand kneading is wonderfully therapeutic. However, if you are likely to be making large quantities of yeast dough regularly, a powerful electric mixer fitted with a dough hook (which I use regularly for batches based on around 3 lb/1.4 kg/12 cups flour) makes light work of it. Smaller quantities are easily made by hand, although hand-held electric mixers usually have dough hooks too; food processors can also be used for small batches. The methods given in the following recipes are interchangeable.

Yeast is a living organism which requires moisture, food and warmth to become active. Particularly sensitive to temperature, it requires gentle warmth to grow and make the dough rise, then the shock of a hot oven to stop the growth and prevent over-rising; this produces bread with a greater volume but a tough texture and a lot of large holes.

The recommended temperature range for reasonably fast rising is about 25-30°C/ 80-85°F — typically the back of a range, a warming oven, gas oven with just the pilot light on, the bottom shelf of an airing cupboard, or on a rack over a pan of simmering water. As moisture is an advantage, you can prevent the dough from drying out and forming a skin by keeping it covered, or put the bowl or baking tin into a large oiled polythene bag. Yeast doughs will rise at lower temperatures, but more slowly.

Tips for successful yeast bread
*Have the kitchen warm.
*Keep windows and doors closed to avoid draughts.
*Cover the dough with a tea/dish towel whenever it is not being handled.

Further information
For more about yeast and types of flour see 'Useful Information'.

Note for American cooks
As a general rule, use 1 package active dry yeast for every 3 lb of flour. For fresh yeast, 1 package = ⅗ oz or 2 tablespoons. However, it is best to check the directions on the package before baking. For this reason, yeast amounts in the following recipes do not have American conversions and are given in ounces and grams only.

Moyglare Yeast Bread

At Moyglare Manor near Maynooth in Co. Kildare, they make a variety of fresh baked goods every day, including this delicious yeast bread. A good example of the original yeast-baking method, it uses fresh yeast, strong flour with a high gluten content, and a small proportion of butter for the best flavour and texture. Bread like this keeps very well. It can be baked in shapes on a baking sheet or in tins. Makes 4 or 5 small loaves.

> 1½ oz/40g fresh yeast
> water, as required (see method)
> 2 oz/50g/½ stick butter
> 1 oz/25g/1 US tbsp salt
> 1 oz/25g/1 US tbsp sugar
> 3 lb/1.4 kg/12 cups strong white flour (bread flour)
> beaten egg, to glaze

Put the yeast into a small bowl with about 4 fl oz/100 ml/½ cup tepid water and leave for 10 minutes, until frothy. Meanwhile, place the butter, salt and sugar into 7 fl oz/200 ml/⅔ cup hot water and leave until the butter has melted.

Put the flour in a mixing bowl. Add the yeast and butter mixtures, and enough warm water to make a stiff dough — the quantity varies according to the absorbency of the flour, but the total liquid in a 3 lb/1.4 kg batch is usually about 1¼ -1½ pints/750-900 ml/3-3¾ cups.

Knead well until no longer sticky, then leave in a warm place and allow to rise once. When the volume has doubled, turn onto a floured worktop. Knock it back, knead again and weigh into 1 lb/450g pieces. Shape into loaves (or put into greased 1 lb/450g loaf tins). Then put the loaves into a warm place to rise again.

Preheat a very hot oven, 500°F/250°C/gas 9. When the loaves have risen again, brush with beaten egg and put them into the prepared oven. Immediately reduce the temperature to fairly hot, 400°F/200°C/gas 6. Bake for about ½ hour, until the loaves are well-risen and golden. They are ready when the base sounds hollow when tapped with the knuckles. Turn out and cool on a wire rack.

Mighty White Dough

At Marlfield House near Gorey in Co. Wexford, they take pride in presenting a selection of breads, including this recipe which contains mixed grains. A small proportion of granary (coarse) flour is included and oil is used instead of butter.

> 1 oz/25g fresh yeast
> generous ½ pint/350 ml/1¼ cups tepid water
> 1 lb 5 oz/585g/4¼ cups strong white bread flour
> 3½ oz/85g/¾ cup granary flour
> ¾ oz/20g/scant 1 US tbsp salt
> 4 tbsp/60 ml/5 US tbsp vegetable oil

Preheat a very hot oven, 450°F/230°C/gas 8, during the second proving.
Blend the yeast with the warm water in a jug or bowl and leave in a warm place

to froth up. Mix the dry ingredients in a mixing bowl, or in the bowl of a mixer fitted with a dough hook. Make a well in the middle. Blend the oil into the yeast and water mixture, pour into the centre of the flour and mix well. Knead until a smooth, elastic dough is formed. (If using a mixer, the dough will leave the sides of the bowl clean and form a ball around the dough hook when it is ready.)

Cover the bowl with a damp tea/dish towel and leave in a warm place to rise. When doubled in size, turn out and knock back to its original size and knead again. The dough can now be shaped to make loaves, rolls or whatever. After shaping as required, preheat the oven and put the dough in a warm place to rise again. Then bake according to chosen size and type, until well-risen and golden-brown.

Coopershill Wholemeal Bread

At Coopershill, Brian and Lindy O'Hara's lovely house in Co. Sligo, Lindy uses a mixture of flours as well as dried yeast in her wholemeal bread. Strong flour is included, along with butter or white fat to improve the texture. This recipe skips the 'creaming' of yeast and sugar, but goes through the whole routine of kneading/fermentation/knocking back/proving. Although time-consuming, this develops the gluten and results in a moist, springy dough which will rise and keep well. Makes 2 small loaves.

8 oz/225g/2 cups wholemeal (whole-wheat) flour
8 oz/225g/2 cups malted brown flour
8 oz/225g/2 cups strong white flour
1 tsp/1¼ US tsp salt
1 oz/25g/¼ stick butter or white fat (lard)
16 fl oz/475 ml/2 cups tepid water
1 tbsp/1¼ US tbsp soft brown sugar
1 sachet (7g) dried yeast

Grease two 1 lb/450g loaf tins. Mix the flours, salt and butter together. Add water, sugar and yeast and combine into a dough. Knead on a floured board for about 7 minutes, until pliable and elastic. Place in a large oiled bowl, cover with a damp tea/dish towel and leave in a warm place until twice its size. Knead again for about 5 minutes. Then divide the dough between the greased tins and leave to rise again.

Meanwhile, preheat a very hot oven, 450°F/230°C/gas 8. When the dough has doubled in size again, bake for about 30 minutes, or until the bread shrinks a little from the sides of the tins and sounds hollow when rapped on the base after turning out. Cool on a wire rack.

Brown Bread with Olive Oil

Down at the Oystercatcher, Bill and Sylvia Patterson's pretty waterside cottage restaurant near Kinsale, Bill — who is from Scotland — is doing something different with this bread. He uses mixed grains, black treacle/molasses and oil for interesting texture and flavour. There is a high proportion of strong flour, fresh yeast and no short cuts in the method, ensuring well-developed gluten and a good springy texture and keeping qualities. Makes the equivalent of 2 large (2 lb/900g) or 4 small (1 lb/900g) loaves.

  2 lb 3 oz/1 kg/8¾ cups strong bread flour
  9 oz/250g/2¼ cups coarse wholemeal flour
  4 oz/100g/1 cup rye flour
  1 oz/25g/2 US tbsp wheat germ
  1 oz/25g/2 US tbsp oat bran
  1 oz/25g/2 US tbsp organic porridge oats
  1 tbsp/1¼ US tbsp salt
  1¼ oz/35g fresh yeast
  1¾ pints/1 litre/4½ cups tepid water
  2½ tbsp/3 US tbsp black treacle (molasses), warmed
  olive oil, as required, for brushing

Mix all the dry ingredients together. Dissolve the yeast with a little of the warm water and add the warmed treacle/molasses and the remaining water. Warm the dry ingredients for a minute in the oven/microwave, then add the warm yeast/treacle mixture. Mix well and knead by hand for 10 minutes, or for 5 minutes if using a mixer with a dough hook.

When the dough comes cleanly away from the bowl and is no longer sticky, brush the surface with olive oil and leave it to prove at room temperature for 1 to 2 hours, until doubled in volume. Knock back to its original size and knead for another 3 minutes, then leave to rest for 10 minutes. Shape or mould into long bread sticks or another preferred shape. Transfer to an oiled baking sheet and put in a warm place to rise again for about 30 minutes, until doubled in volume.

Meanwhile, preheat a very hot oven, 450°F/230°C/gas 8. Bake for about 20-27 minutes, or until crisp and brown.

Erriseask Baguettes

At Erriseask House Hotel and Restaurant at Ballyconneely, Connemara, Stefan Matz is out on his own when it comes to developing gluten. Not content with the usual process, he repeats the kneading process every 15 minutes for an hour to produce that special continental texture. Professional bakers would also steam-bake the bread in a combination oven as he does, but a similar effect is obtained by sprinkling the dough with water before baking in a very hot oven, producing a very light, crisp loaf. Stefan uses only strong white flour, plenty of salt and a higher than usual proportion of fresh yeast to make his baguettes.

1½ oz/40g/1½ US tbsp salt
3lb 4 oz/1.5 kg/13 cups strong white flour
7 fl oz/200 ml/⅔ cup tepid water
2½ oz/60g fresh yeast
1¼-1½ pints /700-900ml/3-3¾ cups tepid water

Put the salt into a mixing bowl, then add the flour on top. Dissolve the yeast in 7 fl oz/200 ml/⅔ cup warm water and mix slightly with a little flour. Wait 10 minutes, then add the yeast mixture to the flour with about 1¼ pints/700 ml/ 3 cups water and mix to a smooth dough, adding more water if necessary. Leave it to rest for 10 minutes, then knead the dough gently. Repeat the kneading every 15 minutes, three times. Set a very hot oven to preheat at 475°F/240°C/gas 9 before the last kneading. Shape the dough into even-sized baguettes (or rolls). Then place on greased and floured baking trays and leave to rest for 10 minutes.

To bake, sprinkle with water and bake for 8 minutes. Then turn the trays around to ensure even cooking. Reduce the temperature to 425°F/210°C/gas 7 and bake for a further 10-12 minutes, until golden-brown and very crisp. The baguettes may need to be turned over for the last few minutes.

Quick & Easy Whole-wheat Bread

At Ballyvolane in Co. Cork, Merrie Greene's kitchen is the heart of the house where she regularly bakes this bread for guests. This recipe demonstrates a move away from conventional yeast cookery, as the flour used is all whole-wheat, the mixture is fatless and the dough is only left to rise once, in the tin. Although dried yeast is used, it is the older type and activated in the same way as fresh yeast, by frothing up with sugar and warm water. Although you can do the kneading with the dough hook of an electric whisk or in a mixer, this is the therapeutic, hand-kneaded version. Makes 1 large or 2 small loaves.

1 lb/450g/4 cups stone-ground whole-wheat flour
2 tsp/2½ US tsp salt
12-13 fl oz/355-380 ml/1½ - 1¾ cups tepid water (approx.)
1 tsp/1¼ US tsp brown sugar
2 level tsp/2½ US tsp dried yeast
a little extra flour, for sprinkling
4 level tsp/5 US tsp sesame seeds

First, weigh the flour and mix the salt through it until fairly evenly distributed. Then warm the flour a little in a low oven for about 10 minutes.

Meanwhile, prepare the yeast by pouring 3 fl oz/75 ml/4 US tbsp of the warm water into a measuring jug, then stir in the sugar and sprinkle in the yeast. Stir once, then leave for 10-15 minutes until a good inch (2.5 cm) of froth has formed.

Tip the warm flour into a large mixing bowl and make a well in the centre. Stir the yeast mixture once (to ensure it has fully dissolved). Then pour it into the well and, starting with a wooden spoon, begin to mix the yeast liquid into the flour to form a dough, gradually adding the rest of the measured water. (The exact amount of water you need depends on the flour.) Finish off the mixing with your hands until you have a smooth dough that leaves the bowl clean, with no bits of flour or dough sticking to the side.

Now transfer the dough to the tin by stretching it out to an oblong and folding one edge into the centre and the other over that. Fit the dough into the tin, pressing all round the edges so that the surface is already slightly rounded. Sprinkle with a generous amount of flour and the sesame seeds. Then cover with a damp tea/dish towel and leave in a warm place to rise for 30-40 minutes, or at room temperature for about 1 hour.

Meanwhile, preheat a hot oven, 400°F/200°C/gas 6. When the dough has risen to within ¼"/½ cm of the top of the tin, bake for 35-45 minutes, depending on the size of the loaf. Then turn out the bread and return to the oven, upside down, for a further 5-10 minutes to crisp the sides and base. Cool on a wire rack.

Quick Wholemeal Yeast Bread

My own everyday wholemeal yeast bread is a compromise between the various methods, as it is kneaded but has only one rising, in the tin. Milk and water are used rather than the usual plain water. The texture and flavour are better if fresh yeast and white vegetable fat or butter are used. This version is particularly simple and takes very little time or attention. Varying the proportion of flours also affects the flavour, size and texture of the bread. If preferred, use 1-1½ oz/25-40g fresh yeast and 2 teaspoons soft dark brown sugar instead of the dried yeast. Makes four 1 lb/450g loaves.

> 2 lb/900g/8 cups fine wholemeal flour
> l lb/450g/4 cups strong white flour
> 3 rounded tsp/3¾ US tsp salt
> 3 sachets easy-blend/fast-action dried yeast
> l pint/600 ml/2½ cups milk, made up to 1¾ pints/l litre/4 ½ cups
>   with boiling water
> 3 tbsp/3¾ US tbsp sunflower or groundnut oil

Mix flours, salt and yeast well in the bowl of a mixer. Measure milk, hot water and oil into a separate jug. Using a dough hook, start on a low speed and gradually add the tepid oil, milk and water mixture. When the liquid has been absorbed into the flour and is unlikely to splash, increase to a medium speed (3) and mix until the dough forms a ball around the dough hook, leaving the sides of the bowl clean. If the mixture seems too wet, sprinkle a little extra flour down the side of the bowl; if too dry, add a little extra liquid — the absorbency rate of flour varies, so the measured amounts aren't always quite right. (If you aren't using a mixer, mix by hand in a large bowl until manageable, then turn out onto a floured work surface and knead until a smooth, elastic ball of dough is formed.)

Turn the dough out onto a floured worktop and knead lightly. Then quarter the ball and knead each piece individually until smooth. Form into oblong shapes and put into four oiled l lb/450g loaf tins, pressing well into the corners. Leave in a warm place for about 20-30 minutes to rise. Preheat a very hot oven, 450°F/230°C/gas 8. When the dough is coming over the tops of the tins, transfer to the centre of the hot oven and bake for 30-40 minutes, until well browned and shrinking slightly from the tins. The bases should sound hollow when tapped. Take the loaves out of the tins for the last 5 or 10 minutes of baking if you like a crisp crust. Cool on a wire rack.

Variations

Using this basic recipe, divide the mixture into three instead of four and make any of the following variations.

*Cheese Bread

To one-third of the basic dough add: 8 oz/225g/2 cups grated mature Cheddar cheese; pinch of mustard powder; 1 beaten egg. Work the cheese, mustard and egg into the dough. Place the dough in a lightly greased large loaf tin (2 lb/900g). Leave to rise and bake as above.

*Garlic Bread

To one-third of the basic bread dough add: 3 cloves garlic, crushed in a little salt. Knead the crushed garlic into the dough and continue as above. Serve hot with soups and salads.

*Herb Bread

To one-third of the basic bread dough add a choice of preferred herbs (or a mixture) such as: 2 tsp oregano; 1½ tsp rosemary; 1 tsp turmeric; or ½ tsp sage. Knead the herb(s) into the dough until evenly distributed, then continue as above.

Basic White Yeast Dough

The quality and range of baking at Gregans Castle, an imposing country house hotel in the Burren in Co. Clare, is impressive. This is a recipe based entirely on strong flour, using conventional dried yeast which is activated in the same way as fresh yeast. Although there is no fat, this dough goes through the full process and is kneaded twice, so the gluten is thoroughly developed to make a well-textured springy loaf.

> 2 lb 3 oz/1 kg/heaped 8 cups strong white flour
> 25g dried yeast
> pinch of salt
> good 1 pint/650 ml/2½ cups tepid water
> beaten egg, or egg and water, to glaze

Preheat a hot oven, 425°F/220°C/gas 7 during the second proving.

Place flour, yeast and salt in a bowl and mix well. Add the warm water and mix to a dough in a mixer or by hand. Knead until the dough is no longer sticky but becomes elastic and forms a ball. Cover it with a damp tea/dish towel and leave it in a warm place until doubled in size. Then turn it out onto a floured work surface and knock back to its original size. The dough is now ready for shaping and can be varied by the addition of herbs, nuts, fruits or spices. Suggestions for shaping could include:

> *Divide the dough into 3. Roll into 3 long sausage shapes and plait/braid together.
> *Roll out the dough to a thickness of ½ "/1.2 cm and roll up as for a roulade.
> *Roll out the dough into one long sausage, then roll around into a circle.
> *Cut the dough into 12 pieces and shape into smooth rolls.

Place the shaped dough on a floured baking tray and leave in a warm place to rise again until doubled in size. Brush with egg and bake in the hot oven, until golden-brown, well-risen and crusty. The flavour will improve if the bread is brushed with melted butter about 3 minutes before removing from the oven.

Malty Brown Bread

This superb, moist bread is from Aherne's Seafood Bar in Youghal, Co. Cork. It is made with fresh yeast, and although the yeast and treacle/molasses give it an excellent flavour, it contains no 'strong' flour or fat and involves no kneading. This makes it closer to the soda bread tradition in terms of method and final texture. It is also cooked at a lower temperature than most breads, which probably explains its exceptional moistness. Makes 1 loaf.

> 1 lb/450g/4 cups wholemeal (whole-wheat) flour
> pinch of salt
> 1 oz/25g fresh yeast
> 1 dsp/1½ US tbsp black treacle (molasses)
> ¾ pint/450 ml/2 cups tepid water (approx.)

Mix the flour and salt and put in a warm place. Mix the yeast, treacle/molasses and half of the tepid water in a jug and allow to ferment (froth up). When the yeast rises, rub the yeast mixture into the flour and add enough tepid water to make a moist dough. Turn into an oiled loaf tin and allow the dough to rise.

Meanwhile, preheat a moderate oven, 350°F/180°C/gas 4.

When the dough has risen to about twice its original size, bake for 45 minutes. Then turn out of the tin and bake for another 10 minutes, or until the bread sounds hollow when tapped. Wrap in a tea/dish towel on a wire rack to cool. (This makes a soft crust.)

Note: There is no need to multiply the yeast in direct proportions for larger batches of bread. For a 3 lb/1.4 kg/12 cup batch, for example, 1½- 2 oz/40-50g fresh yeast should be enough.

Crookedwood House Wholemeal Loaf

A moist, nutty loaf, with no kneading. Makes 1 loaf.

> ¾ pint/450 ml/2 cups tepid water
> 2 tbsp/2½ US tbsp dark soft brown sugar
> 1 sachet dried yeast
> 1 lb/450g/4 cups wholemeal flour
> fistful of bran
> 1 tsp/1¼ US tsp salt
> sesame seeds

Pour ⅔ of the water into a large mixing bowl. Add the sugar and sprinkle the yeast on top, then put it in a warm place. Grease a 2 lb/900g loaf tin and leave it to warm.

Measure the flour into a separate bowl and mix in the bran and salt. When the yeast is frothing up, give the mixture a stir and add the flour, bran and salt, with the remaining water. Mix well to make a wet dough. Add a little extra water if necessary — the consistency should be much too wet to knead. Pour the mixture into the greased loaf tin, sprinkle with sesame seeds and leave it to prove in a warm place for about 50 minutes After about 30 minutes, preheat a very hot oven, 450°F/230°C/gas 8. When the dough has risen to double its original size, bake for about 45 minutes, until crisp and shrinking slightly from the sides of the tin. Turn out and cool on a wire rack.

Treacle Bread

This dark, delicious and moist bread is made at Le Château in Athlone. Except that easy-blend yeast is used and the mixture includes some white flour (although not specifically 'strong' bakers' flour), this recipe represents a development of method similar to the previous one: no fat and no kneading. It produces a loaf with the nutty texture more typical of soda breads but with a more complex flavour. This quantity makes 8 small loaves; half quantities may suit most households better, although it freezes well.

4 lb/1.8 kg/16 cups stone-ground wholemeal (whole-wheat) flour
2 lb/900g/8 cups white flour
4 oz/100g/4 US tbsp caster sugar
1 oz/25g/1 US tbsp salt
6 sachets easy-mix dried yeast
4 tbsp/60 ml/5 US tbsp treacle (molasses)
3 pints/1.8 litres/7½ cups tepid warm water

Lightly grease eight 1 lb/450g loaf tins.

Place the wholemeal flour in a large bowl. Sift all the other dry ingredients together (including the yeast) and add to the wholemeal flour. Mix well. Add treacle/molasses, mixed with some of the warm water. Then mix in the rest of the warm water to make a wet dough. (The exact amount varies, depending on the absorbency of the flour.)

When thoroughly mixed, half fill the prepared tins and leave for about 40 minutes or until fully risen. Meanwhile, preheat a hot oven, 425°F/220°C/gas 7. When the dough has doubled in size, put into the oven, then reduce the temperature to 375°F/190°C/gas 5. Bake for about 1 hour, until the loaves are shrinking slightly from their tins and the bread sounds hollow when tapped on the base. Cool on wire racks.

Max's Brown Bread

Max's Wine Bar in Kinsale makes a bread which is a darkly sweet and moist. It contains treacle and syrup, with a higher than usual proportion of fresh yeast, but no fat. They've been making this characterful bread at their charming restaurant for years and say it is based on the famous 'Ballymaloe Brown Bread' which, in turn, is a version of the 'Grant Loaf', developed by Doris Grant in the 1930s — an unusually clear line of descent and an interesting example of the way recipes gradually change. It's important to have all ingredients and equipment at hand-warm temperature. The texture of the dough should be just too wet to knead. Makes four 2 lb/900g loaves.

3 ½ lb/1.6 kg/14 cups wholemeal (whole-wheat) flour
1 tbsp/1¼ US tbsp salt
1-2 rounded tbsp/1¼-2½ US tbsp black treacle (molasses)
2 tbsp/2½ US tbsp golden (Karo) syrup
2½ pints/1.5 litres/6 cups tepid water
4 oz/100g fresh yeast (from the baker)

Mix the flour with the salt and warm in the oven, set at its lowest temperature. In a small bowl, mix the treacle/molasses and syrup with some of the water and crumble in the yeast. Put the bowl in a warm place to activate the yeast.

Grease 4 large loaf tins (2 lb/900g) and put them to warm.

The yeast should be frothing up after about 5 minutes. Stir it well, then add the remaining water and mix with the flour to make a wet dough. Divide the mixture between the tins, cover with a warm, clean tea/dish towel and put back into a warm place again. Set the oven at 450°F/230°C/gas 8 to preheat while the bread rises.

After about 20 minutes, when the dough has doubled in size, put the loaves into the hot oven and bake for 45-50 minutes, until well-risen and crisp. When ready, the loaves will shrink slightly from their tins and sound hollow if tapped on the base after turning out. Cool on a wire rack.

Brown Yeast Bread with Mixed Grains

This is made by Helen Mullane and Armel Whyte at Allo's, their Listowel bistro. It's another good example of an Irish hybrid bread, a mixture of the yeast- and soda-baking traditions. It includes a small proportion of strong white flour but also an interesting mixture of grains. Although fresh yeast is used, the mixture is not kneaded, but put straight into the tin to rise. The flavour will be richer and more subtle, but the texture will be more like soda bread than true yeast bread, as the gluten in the flours is not fully developed by the kneading process. Makes one 2 lb/900g loaf.

> 8 oz/225g/2 cups wholemeal (whole-wheat) flour
> 4 oz/100g/1 cup strong white flour
> 4 oz/100g/⅔ cup mixed bran, pinhead oatmeal and wheat germ
> 1 tsp/1¼ US tsp salt
> 1 oz/25g fresh yeast
> 1 pint/600 ml/2½ cups tepid water
> 2 tsp/2½ US tsp black treacle (molasses)

Grease a 2 lb/900g loaf tin.

Combine the flours with the grain mixture and salt in a mixing bowl. Put in a warm place.

In a bowl or jug, mix the yeast with the tepid water and treacle; leave in a warm place. When the yeast has frothed up, add the liquids to the warmed mixed flour. Stir well, then turn the mixture into the greased loaf tin, to about half full. Leave in a warm place again to rise. Meanwhile, preheat a very hot oven, 450°F/230°C/gas 8.

When the mixture reaches the top of the tin, place it in the hot oven. After 10 minutes, reduce the temperature to moderate, 350°F/180°C/gas 4 and cook for a further 40 minutes, until the loaf shrinks away from the sides of the tin a little and sounds hollow when tapped on the base. Cool on a wire rack.

Wholemeal Health Bread

Rosemarie Kennan's bread, from Roundwood House in Co. Laois, is a most interesting recipe from the 'super-hybrid' category. Although it is a fresh yeast recipe, and a kneaded one at that, the methods of handling, shaping and baking the dough owe as much to the Irish soda bread tradition as to yeast cookery. The ingredients include elements of both traditions, with buttermilk (or yogurt) as well as the fresh yeast, but no fat. For good measure, Rosemarie includes some sultanas/dried green grapes and even tahini. She says she prefers to bake it in a cast-iron pot (an echo of the old 'bastible' pot-oven), making this a real one-off. Makes 1 round loaf.

> 1½ lb/700g/6 cups wholemeal (whole-wheat) flour
> 1 tsp/1¼ US tsp salt
> 2 tbsp/2½ US tbsp tepid water
> 3 tsp/3¾ US tsp fresh yeast
> 2 fl oz/50 ml/scant ¼ cup milk
> 2 tbsp/2½ US tbsp black treacle (molasses)
> 1 tbsp/1½ US tbsp honey
> 3 oz/75g/⅔ cup sultanas (dried green grapes)
> ½ pint/300 ml/1¼ cups buttermilk or natural yogurt
> 1 tbsp/1¼ US tbsp tahini (sesame seed paste)

Combine the flour and salt. Dilute the yeast in the warm water and add to the flour mixture. In a saucepan, warm the milk over gentle heat and add the treacle/molasses and honey. Stir to melt, then add the sultanas.

Cool this mixture. Then add it, with the buttermilk or yogurt and the tahini, to the flour and yeast mixture. Knead by hand or use an electric mixer fitted with a dough hook, on low speed. When the dough is smooth and no longer sticks to the bowl, cover the bowl with a tea/dish towel and leave it in a warm place for 1 hour.

Preheat a fairly hot oven, 375°F/190°C/gas 5.

Knead again for 1 minute, then roll the dough out on a floured board to form a circle 1½ "/3.8 cm deep. Place the loaf on a floured baking sheet and cut a large cross in the top with a floured knife. Bake for 40 minutes.

Rosemarie herself bakes the loaf in an old cast-iron cooking pot with a lid to give a softer crust.

Blue Haven Brown Bread

Seafood is the speciality at Brian and Anne Cronin's Blue Haven Hotel in the picturesque seaside town of Kinsale, Co. Cork. Large quantities of brown bread are baked daily to accompany dishes like the hearty chowders on the bar menu and smoked salmon and shellfish in the restaurant. Alongside a crusty soda bread, this wholemeal yeast bread containing fresh yeast and treacle is always on offer. It's a rich and flavoursome compromise between the soda and yeast traditions. Makes 1 large or 2 small loaves.

> 1 lb/450g/4 cups wholemeal flour
> 2 tsp/2½ US tsp salt
> 1 tsp/1¼ US tsp black treacle (molasses)
> 1 oz/25g fresh yeast
> 12 fl oz/350 ml/1½ cups tepid water

Mix the flour with the salt and set it to warm in a cool oven.

Mix the treacle/molasses with a little of the water in a small bowl and crumble in the yeast; leave the bowl in a warm position such as the back of the cooker.

Grease one large or two small loaf tins and put them into a warm place, along with a clean tea/dish towel.

After about 45 minutes, the yeast should be frothing up. Stir it well and mix it with the remaining warm water. Mix it with the warmed flour to make a fairly wet dough and put it into the greased warmed tin(s). Return to the position previously used to activate the yeast and cover with the warm tea/dish towel.

Preheat a very hot oven, 470°F/230°C/gas 8.

After about 20 minutes, the dough will have doubled in size. Bake in the centre of the hot oven for 45-50 minutes, until nicely browned and sounding hollow when tapped. Cool on a wire rack.

Variation

Dried yeast may be used instead, but use only half the weight given (1 sachet, if using fast-action/easy-blend) and allow longer to rise.

Speciality Breads

The 'Mediterranean diet' swept the board a few years ago. At more or less the same time, chefs everywhere (notably Johnny Cooke of Cooke's Cafe in Dublin, who spear-headed the new movement) seemed to find inspiration in the colour and sun-filled flavours of Mediterranean and Cal-Ital foods. Since then, there has been a rush towards all sorts of 'new wave' breads, with every little restaurant seeming to produce continental bread and olive oil dips.

How many will still be making such things in ten years' time remains to be seen, but for the moment, it is a lively and exciting phase, so a small selection of the country's best is included here. Other speciality breads are an exceptional continental fruit bread which is a dream with Irish farmhouse cheese, an unusual Italian dough that can also be used as a pizza base, and a few quick and easy recipes for holiday baking.

Light White Yeast Bread

At Bully's Restaurant and Wine Bar in Cork, they make a most wonderful bread which seems to break all the rules: it uses strong white flour, fresh yeast, oil (a lot) and a milk and water mix. While it is unkneaded, it is still very elastic. Eugene Buckley says the secret of this bread's lightness lies in careful, light handling — although they use a mixer for the initial stage when making catering-size batches, everything else is done by hand. The bread is baked in long, narrow tins (about 12"x4"/30.5cm/10cm), but it could also be baked successfully in ordinary loaf tins. Makes 2 long loaves.

> 1½ lb/700g/6 cups strong white flour
> ½ oz/15g fresh yeast
> ½ oz/15g/1 US tsp salt
> ½ teacup (about 2½ fl oz/65 ml/¼ cup) tepid milk
> l tbsp/1¼ US tbsp sugar
> l teacup (about 5 fl oz/150 ml/½ cup) oil
> l pint/600 ml/2½ cups tepid water

Preheat a very hot oven, 450°F/230°C/gas 8.

Mix flour, yeast, salt, milk and sugar together to make a batter. Add the oil and mix again. Then add enough water to make a wet dough. Mix thoroughly and throw out onto a floured worktop. Cut into rough shapes (2 if using the special tins, probably 4 for domestic loaf tins) and leave to rise.

When roughly doubled in size, roll the dough lightly in your hands and put into oiled tins, pressing lightly into the sides and corners. Cover with a warm towel and leave in a warm place to rise again until just over the top of the tin — the dough will be feather-light when ready to go into the oven.

Bake for 30-40 minutes, until the bread is shrinking slightly from the tin and sounds hollow when tapped. Turn out and cool on a wire rack.

Note: *Although it can be hard to handle, this dough also makes an exceptionally light pizza base. Beware of over-handling, as this will make the bread/pizza tough.*

Quay House Flat Bread

At Destry Rides Again, Paddy and Julia Foyle's wacky little Clifden restaurant, chef Dermot Gannon was well in the advance guard of the trend towards Mediterranean food. He makes a delicious olive bread called simply 'Flat Bread'. The method is conventional but it's simple to make using 'easy-blend' dried yeast — and of course it has a thoroughly Mediterranean character in appearance and flavour. Makes 1 loaf.

> 1 lb/450g/4 cups strong white flour
> 1 sprig of rosemary
> 6 leaves of basil
> 10 pitted black olives
> 3 tsp/3¾ US tsp 'easy-mix' dried yeast
> 10 sun-dried tomatoes, chopped
> tepid water, to mix
> sea salt, to sprinkle

Opposite:
Bee's Brown
Bread, perfect
with cheese
and chutney
at Tinakilly
House in
Co. Wicklow
(page 4)

Previous page:
An enticing
selection of
breads from
Gregans Castle
(page 47)

An appetising array for afternoon tea at Gregans Castle, Co. Clare (page 47)

A lovely nutty bread – Mixed Grain & Yogurt Loaf (page 8)

Flower Crêpes with Summer Berry Filling, one of Linda Saunders' floral delights at the Old Rectory (page 25)

Opposite:
Irish Tea Cake from Coopershill House – a cross between a brack and a fruit cake (page 31)

American Banana Bread, always on the dessert trolly at Blairs Cove (page 37)

Opposite: At Ballymaloe House, the Fruit Soda Bread is called 'Spotted Dog' (page 30)

Next page: There's a Mediterranean flair in the Quay House Flat Bread (page 54)

Pancakes with Apple & Ginger Marmalade – old traditions meet the new at Crookedwood House (page 22)

'Mighty White' (page 42) and other bread delights from Marlfield House

Place flour, herbs, olives and dried yeast in a large bowl. Add the chopped tomatoes and make a well in the centre. Mix in enough tepid water to make a soft dough. Cover and leave in a warm place until doubled in size. Then remove from the bowl, turn out onto a floured work surface and knead for about 5 minutes. Place on an oiled tray and flatten. Brush with olive oil and sprinkle with sea salt. Leave to rise again for 15 minutes.

Meanwhile, preheat a very hot oven, 400°F/200°C/gas 6. Bake for about 15 minutes, until brown, crisp and hollow when tapped on the base.

Hint: If sun-dried tomatoes are unavailable, try drying fresh tomatoes by placing in a very low oven, such as the bottom oven of an Aga, and leaving for about 12 hours.

Rathsallagh Tomato & Cheese Bread

This is baked in loaf tins and, although distinctly Mediterranean in character, Kay O'Flynn's variation is interesting. 'Easy-blend' yeast is used and the mixture is only kneaded once, but when the dough is in the tins, they are put into oiled polythene bags and left at room temperature. This much slower method of rising the dough compensates for a reduced amount of kneading and allows the gluten in the flour longer to develop, producing a better texture — and backing up the theory that the more slowly yeast works on dough, the better the bread will be. Makes 2 1lb/450g loaves.

> 1½ lb/700g/6 cups strong white flour
> 1 dsp/1½ US tbsp salt
> 1 sachet easy-blend dried yeast
> 5 oz/150g/1 cup hard cheese, grated
> 5 fl oz/150 ml/½ cup olive or salad oil
> 13 fl oz/375ml/1½ cups warm water
> 3 tbsp/45 ml/3¾ US tbsp tomato purée
> 3 cloves garlic, crushed
> pinch of cayenne pepper
> 2 oz black olives, stoned and chopped

Sift the flour into a large bowl and mix in the salt and yeast. Then add the grated cheese. Mix the oil, water, tomato purée, crushed garlic and cayenne together and add to the flour mixture. Mix with a wooden spoon to make a firm dough. Turn out onto a lightly floured work surface and knead for about 5 minutes until the dough feels elastic.

Oil two 1 lb/450g loaf tins and divide the dough between them. Put into polythene bags and leave to rise in a draught-free place at room temperature for about 4 hours. Preheat a hot oven, 450°F/220°C/gas 8.

When the dough has doubled in size, stud the tops of the loaves gently with the chopped olives. Bake for 10 minutes, then reduce the temperature to 400°F/200°C/gas 6 for another 20 minutes. Turn onto a wire rack to cool.

Variation

Top the loaves with 2 thinly sliced tomatoes and reserve a little of the grated cheese to sprinkle over.

Caragh Lodge Onion Bread

At her lovely country house overlooking Caragh Lake on the Ring of Kerry, Mary Gaunt bakes all kinds of tempting things for her guests. This moist, savoury bread, made with strong flour and fresh yeast, is kneaded well to develop the gluten. It has an excellent texture and good keeping qualities and is especially delicious with home-made soup. Makes 3 small loaves.

   1 oz/25g fresh yeast
   1 tsp/1¼ US tsp sugar
   1 pint/600 ml/2½ cups warm milk and water
   2 lb/900g/8 cups strong flour
   1 coffee spoon/⅛ US tsp salt
   8 oz/225g/2 cups Cheddar cheese, grated
   4 cloves garlic, crushed
   1 tbsp parsley, chopped
   1 oz/25g/¼ stick butter
   4 large onions, roughly sliced

Put the yeast and sugar into a bowl and add the warm liquid. Mix until quite smooth. Cover with a cloth and put to rise in a warm place.

   Meanwhile, sift the flour and salt into a large bowl. Add the grated cheese, crushed garlic and parsley. Melt the butter in a pan and gently sauté the onions in it until soft but not browned, then add to the dry ingredients. When the yeast mixture has frothed up, add it to the dry ingredients. Mix well, then turn out onto a floured work surface and knead until smooth. Return to the bowl, cover and put into a warm place to prove.

   When the dough has doubled in size, turn out and knock back. Knead until smooth and elastic. Then divide into 3 pieces and shape. Put into 3 greased 1 lb/450g loaf tins and leave in a warm place to rise. Meanwhile, preheat a hot oven, 425°F/220°C/gas 7.

   When the dough has risen to the top of the tins, bake for about 30 minutes, until golden-brown. Turn out onto a wire rack and leave to cool.

White Bread with Olive Oil & Poppy Seeds

Bill Patterson makes this delicious loaf at The Oystercatcher, his waterside restaurant near Kinsale in Co. Cork. It's a traditional yeast bread using fresh yeast and strong flour — no short cuts — brought into the 'new wave' category by the inclusion of olive oil and poppy seeds. Bill likes to serve it warm and dressed with garlic-flavoured olive oil. The proving time depends on the warmth of the kitchen and will be quicker in summer. Cooking time and yield depend on the size and shape of the loaves.

   ¾ oz/20g fresh yeast
   ¾ oz/20g/scant 1 US tbsp sugar
   scant 1 pint/500 ml/2½ cups warm water
   1½ lb/700g/6 cups strong white bread flour
   1 level tbsp/1¼ US tbsp salt

5 tbsp/6 US tbsp olive oil
poppy seeds and semi-coarse sea salt, to sprinkle

Dissolve the yeast and sugar in the warm water. Sift flour and salt together and warm in the microwave for a minute (longer in a conventional oven). Add the yeast mixture to the dry ingredients and mix well. Knead for 10 minutes by hand, or 5 minutes in a mixer with a dough hook. When the mixture is no longer sticky and comes cleanly away from the bowl to form a ball, brush with olive oil and leave to prove at room temperature for 1 to 2 hours, until doubled in size.

Knock back and leave to rest for 10 minutes. Then shape into long loaves or another preferred shape and slash the top with a sharp knife. Transfer to a baking sheet brushed with olive oil and dusted with flour. Brush the dough with olive oil again and sprinkle with poppy seeds and semi-coarse sea salt. Leave to rise again for another 30-40 minutes.

Meanwhile, preheat a very hot oven, 450°F/230°C/gas 8.

When the dough has doubled in volume again, bake for 20-25 minutes, until crisp and golden-brown. Cool on a wire rack.

Temple House Rye Bread

Percevals have lived at Temple House in Co. Sligo since the mid seventeenth century. One of Ireland's most remarkable country houses, it's an imposing Georgian mansion with a colourful history to match its larger-than-life personality. Despite its size and uncompromising grandeur, there are homely touches, not least in Deb Perceval's good home cooking. Much appreciated by guests, this recipe is interesting in using rye, once an important grain in Ireland which has fallen out of favour in recent years. Rye is a good flour for yeast baking, making a rather tough, chewy bread with a slightly sour flavour that works particularly well with cheese. Here it is mixed with strong white flour and flavoured with pumpkin seeds and orange, although it can also be made plain. Keeps well and makes two 2 lb/900g loaves.

2 oz/50g/½ stick butter
2 oz/50g/2 US tbsp black treacle (molasses)
12 fl oz/350 ml/1½ cups water
1 oz/25g yeast
1 lb/450g/4 cups rye flour
1 lb/450g/4 cups strong stone-ground white flour
1 tsp/1¼ US tsp salt
2 oz/50g/2 US tbsp sunflower or pumpkin seeds
1 tbsp grated rind and the juice of 1 orange
1 small pot (5 fl oz/125 ml) natural yogurt

Melt the butter and treacle/molasses by warming with the water. Then add the yeast and allow it to froth. Mix the flours, salt, seeds and grated orange rind in a separate bowl. Then add the warm yeast liquid, yogurt and orange juice and mix to make a firm dough.

Cover the bowl with a tea/dish towel and leave to rise for 1 hour, or until doubled in size. Knead until smooth. Place in two oiled 2 lb/900g loaf tins and leave to rise again.

Meanwhile, preheat a very hot oven 450°F/230°C/gas 8. Bake for 35 minutes.

BBQ Garlic & Herb Pulled Bread

This is often on the menu at Tony and Alex Daly's bustling restaurant, The Lime Tree, in Kenmare, Co. Kerry. The recipe makes 20 bread rolls or sticks which are made by the 'true' yeast method, then pulled apart when baked, brushed with a garlic and herb paste and charred on a barbecue or charcoal grill.

Basic Dough
good 1 oz/25g fresh yeast
1 dsp/1½ US tbsp sugar
13 fl oz/375 ml/1⅔ cups milk and tepid water
1¼ lb/600g/5 cups strong flour
1 tsp/1¼ US tsp salt
1 oz/25g/¼ stick unsalted butter, melted
egg and water, to glaze

Garlic & Herb Mix
2 tbsp/2½ US tbsp mixed fresh herbs (rosemary, parsley, thyme), chopped
2 cloves garlic, finely crushed
3 tbsp/3¾ US tbsp olive oil
salt, to taste
freshly ground pepper, to taste

To make the basic dough
Mix the yeast with the sugar and dissolve in half of the tepid milk and water. Sift flour and salt into a mixing bowl and make a well in the centre. Add the yeast mixture, melted butter and the rest of the tepid milk and water. Mix and knead to make a smooth dough, adjusting the texture with extra flour or liquid, as required. Cover with a tea/dish towel and leave in a warm place until doubled in size. Then knock back, shape into rolls or sticks and lay out on greased baking sheets to rise again.

Meanwhile, preheat a hot oven, 425°F/220°C/gas 6. When the rolls or bread sticks have doubled in size again, brush them lightly with a mixture of egg and water to glaze and bake for 12-15 minutes, until golden-brown.

To finish on the barbecue
Make a paste with the herbs, garlic, oil and seasoning. Roughly *pull* the rolls apart and brush with the herb mixture. Place them onto the hot barbecue/grill until crisp and blackened. Serve hot.

Old Rectory Marigold & Parsley Bread

Linda Saunders of the Old Rectory in Wicklow is renowned for her creative use of flowers in food. 'Pot marigold (*Calendula*) petals impart a lovely colour and slightly nutty flavour to this easy-to-make white yeast bread. Marigolds have been used as a culinary flower throughout the ages as a substitute for saffron, and both the marigolds and the parsley keep their colour during cooking. As kneading by hand can be difficult, this recipe uses a mixer, making it suitable for older children to cook and enjoy.' This white yeast bread is mixed quickly with easy-blend yeast and only rises once. Linda likes to serve it with chive butter. Makes 2 large loaves.

> 1½ lb/700g/6 cups strong white flour
> 1 sachet quick-action dried yeast
> 2 good pinches of salt
> 2 heaped tsp sugar
> clean, fresh petals of 20 pot marigold heads (not the stamens)
> 2 tbsp/2½ US tbsp parsley, freshly chopped
> 2 tbsp/2½ US tbsp vegetable oil
> 14 fl oz/400 ml/1¾ cups warm water
> 1 egg + extra petals, to brush

Put all the dry ingredients (including the petals and parsley) into the bowl of an electric mixer fitted with a dough hook. Add oil and water and mix for 5 minutes on moderate speed, until the dough becomes elastic and forms a ball around the dough hook. Turn out onto a floured worktop, shape into two loaves and put onto baking trays. Cover with a tea/dish towel and put in a warm place to rise for ½ hour. Preheat a hot oven, 425°F/220°C/gas 7.

When the loaves have doubled in size, glaze with a little whisked egg and sprinkle a few marigold petals over. Bake for 20 minutes, until the loaves are golden-brown and sound hollow when tapped on the base. Remove from the oven and leave to cool on a wire rack.

Continental Fruit Bread

In his kitchen overlooking the white coral strand at Erriseask House Hotel and Restaurant at Ballyconneely in Connemara, Stefan Matz makes this wonderful, dense loaf. It keeps well and is an exceptionally good accompaniment to cheese. Because of the amount of fruit and nuts in the mixture, the yeast content is high. Do not expect an ordinary bread — it should make a close-textured, fruit-packed loaf that can be sliced very thinly. Makes about 4 loaves.

> 3¼ lb/1.5 kg (4 x 375g packs) prunes, stoned
> 13 oz/375g/2 cups dried mixed fruit (sultanas, raisins etc.)
> ½ oz/15g/1 US tsp salt
> 7 oz/200g/1½ cups almonds, (blanched, chopped and roasted)
> 4 oz/100g/⅔ cup shelled walnuts, chopped and roasted
> 7 oz/200g/2 cups mixture of seeds and flours (pumpkin, sunflower,
>   linseeds, oatlets, wheat bran, pinhead oatmeal, stone-ground
>   wholemeal flour)
> 1¼ lb/500g/5 cups strong white unbleached flour
> scant 2 oz/40g fresh yeast
> warm water (see method)

Soak the stoned prunes and dried fruit in 7 fl oz/200 ml/⅔ cup warm water until plump and juicy.

Mix in the salt, nuts and seed-flour mixture and lay the strong white flour on top.

Dissolve the yeast in 7 fl oz/200 ml/⅔ cup warm water and mix with a small quantity of flour. Leave to froth up.

After 15 minutes, add the yeast and mix all the ingredients together to make a moist but firm dough, adding small amounts of water, if required. (It is better to use less water than seems to be needed, as the soaked prunes will gradually give moisture to the mixture.)

Shape the dough into a ball and let it rest in a warm place for 15 minutes, covered with a tea/dish towel. Then knead gently and leave to rest for another 15 minutes. Repeat this twice. Preheat oven, as below.

Shape the dough into rolls or baguettes 2"/5 cm wide. Place on greased baking trays and bake in a preheated fan-assisted oven at 350°F/180°C/gas 4 (conventional oven = 425°F/220°C/gas 7) for 30 minutes. Turn trays around during baking to ensure even browning. Cool on a wire rack.

When cold, wrap tightly in cling-film and store for up to 4 weeks. For longer storage, the bread freezes well and can still be kept for at least a week after thawing. Remove from the freezer about 2 hours before required.

Note: Professionals using a combi-oven could steam for 8 minutes at 100°C/200°F/ gas ¼, then bake for 25 minutes at 350°F/180°C/gas 4 on fan-assisted dry heat. Steaming is optional, however. Temperatures are far less critical than with most breads as a crisp crust is not required and the texture should be close.

Olive Rolls

This simple little recipe can be made even simpler and quicker if the dough is just kneaded once. Add the olives and shape the rolls immediately after the first kneading. Then put straight into the hot oven when they have doubled in size. The texture won't be quite the same, but eat them warm from the oven and nobody will notice. Makes 12 rolls.

> 1 lb/450g/4 cups strong white flour
> 2 tsp/2½ US tsp salt
> 1 sachet easy-mix yeast
> 2 tbsp/2½ US tbsp olive oil
> ½ pint/300 ml/1¼ cups tepid water
> 2 oz/50g black olives, stoned and roughly chopped

Sift the flour and salt together, then add the yeast. Mix well and blend in the olive oil and water. Knead until smooth, then cover with a clean tea/dish towel and leave in a warm place to rise.

When the dough has doubled in volume, turn it out onto a floured surface, knock back to its original size and knead in the chopped olives. Shape into 12 balls. Leave in a warm place to rise for about 15 minutes.

Meanwhile, preheat a fairly hot oven, 400°F/200°C/gas 6. Bake for 15-20 minutes, until brown and crisp.

Walnut Bread

Not all speciality breads have to be made with yeast. This is a long-standing favourite at Dan Mullane's Mustard Seed, his splendid country house and restaurant at Echo Lodge. It contains an impressive array of ingredients for both texture and flavour and is firmly in the soda bread tradition. Makes 4 small (1 lb/450g) loaves.

> 2½ lb/1.1 kg/10 cups wholemeal (whole-wheat) flour
> 3½ oz/90g/⅔ cup wheat germ
> 3½ oz/90g/3 US tbsp pinhead oatmeal
> 3½ oz/90g/⅔ cup bran
> 3½ oz/90g/⅔ cup oat flakes
> 3½ oz/90g/⅔ cup walnuts, chopped
> 2 tsp/2 ½ US tsp bread (baking) soda
> 2 tsp/2 ½ US tsp salt
> 6 oz/175g/1½ sticks unsalted butter, melted
> 2½ fl oz/65g/¼ cup treacle (molasses)
> generous 2½ pints/1.5 litres/6 cups buttermilk

Grease and flour 4 small (1 lb/450g) loaf tins. Preheat a cool oven, 300°F/150°C/gas 2.

Mix the dry ingredients together in a large bowl. Melt the butter, then warm with the treacle until runny and mix in with the buttermilk. Add the liquids to the dry ingredients and blend well to make a wet mixture.

Divide equally between the prepared loaf tins and bake for 3 hours. Turn out onto a wire rack and leave to cool. This bread is hard to cut while it is hot, but it freezes well.

Marmalade Muffins

Also known as 'Mum's Muffins', these are incredibly quick and easy if you have a processor or blender, as they are based on a batter — and they won't make crumbs if you're having breakfast in bed! You need deep bun/muffin tins for this recipe, which is delicious when made with home-made marmalade and just right for a tray of 12 — an ideal treat for overnight guests.

> 3 eggs
> 6 oz/170g/1½ cups plain (all-purpose) flour
> ½ tsp salt
> good ½ pint/300 ml/1¼ cups milk
> l tsp finely grated orange zest
> 1½ tbsp/2 US tbsp melted butter or oil
> 12 tsp marmalade, preferably home-made

Make a batter with the eggs, flour, salt and milk. If using a processor or blender, put the eggs in first so the flour doesn't stick to the bowl and mix until smooth. Add the orange zest and melted butter or oil. Blend again until thoroughly mixed and smooth, with bubbles rising. Pour into a jug, cover and put aside in a cool place until required.

   Preheat a hot oven, 425°F/220°C/gas 7. Grease the deep bun/muffin tins well and put into the oven until really hot. Pour the batter into the cups, filling each one about two-thirds. Then stir a teaspoonful of marmalade into each one (the marmalade can be warmed slightly if it is too stiff). Put straight into the hot oven. After about 10 minutes, reduce the temperature to 350°F/180°C/gas 4 and bake for another 20 minutes, until well-risen and golden-brown. Eat hot with butter and more marmalade, if you like.

Bow Hall Muffins

Bow Hall is set in a lovely garden in Castletownshend, Co. Cork and has to be one of the most delightful B&Bs in the country. Barbara Vickery's delicious American breakfast is a wonder to behold and includes these smashing muffins, served warm and more-ish. In true American style, the raising agent is baking powder, rather than yeast or soda. The cups used are American ones — about the size of a coffee mug. Just keep the proportions right and they'll be fine. Makes 12-16, depending on tin size.

> 1½ cups Bran Buds
> 1¼ cups milk
> 1 egg, lightly beaten
> ⅓ cup sunflower oil
> 1¼ cups flour
> 1 tsp baking powder
> ½ tsp salt
> scant ½ cup sugar
> ½ apple, peeled and cut up finely

Preheat a moderately hot oven, 375°F/190°C/gas 5.

Add the milk to the Bran Buds and leave to soak briefly (a couple of minutes). Mix in the lightly beaten egg and the oil. Sift flour, baking powder and salt together, then stir in the sugar and the chopped apple. Add the liquids to the dry ingredients and stir well to mix. Then beat with a wooden spoon to make a smooth batter. Spoon into greased muffin or deep bun tins, filling them two-thirds full. Bake for about 25 minutes, until golden-brown. Serve immediately.

Irish-American Soda Bread

This recipe, said to have come from Dublin originally and arriving via New Jersey, demonstrates a distinct American influence. The donor, a charming sailing man called Ross Pilling, was lamenting the lack of variety in Irish breads. 'In the States, all sorts of things go into Irish Soda Bread; you'll never see it plain like it is here.' True to his word, he sent me the recipe he uses to bake bread on his boat: 'It may not be kosher, but it is good. This is a versatile bread; you can sweeten it with sugar and fruit or vary its flavour with different grains. The caraway seeds came in particularly handy this year. Everybody loved them — but we also had a few migrant ants in the flour. They look a lot like the Caraway seeds. So unless you look carefully for the little legs, you couldn't tell the difference!' I've called this recipe 'Ross's Little Legs' ever since. Ross's cups are about the size of an average coffee mug. Makes 2 loaves about 8"/20 cm diameter.

    4 cups plain (all-purpose) flour, unsifted
    1 tsp salt
    3 tsp baking powder
    1 tsp baking soda
    ¼ cup sugar (optional)
    3 tsp caraway seeds (optional)
    ⅛ tsp cardamom (optional)
    2 tbsp citron/chopped peel (optional)
    1½ cups raisins
    ¼ cup (2 oz/50g) butter or margarine
    1 egg, lightly beaten
    1¾ cups buttermilk

Preheat a moderately hot oven, 375°F/190°C/gas 5. Grease two 8"/20 cm sandwich tins.

In a large bowl, combine the flour, salt, baking powder, soda, sugar, spices, peel and raisins. Add in the butter or margarine and cut in with a pastry blender or two knives until crumbly. Beat the egg slightly and mix with the buttermilk; add to the dry ingredients and stir until blended. Turn out onto a floured board and knead for 2 or 3 minutes, until smooth.

Divide the dough into 2 pieces and shape into round loaves. Place in the prepared tins and press down until the dough fills the tins. With a sharp knife, cut crosses in the tops of the loaves, about ½"/1.2 cm deep in the middle. Bake for 35-40 minutes, until crisp and hollow-sounding when tapped on the base. Cool on a wire rack and use on the day of baking, if possible.

Barbara's Guinness 'Yeast' Bread

This is probably an American recipe, although it was given to me by an Irish friend who swears by it for easy holiday baking. It can be made with the minimum of equipment and in ovens of varying efficiency. Exact quantities (and oven temperature) are unimportant. Makes 1 loaf.

3 cups plain flour
3 dsp/4 US tbsp baking powder
¼ cup brown sugar
1 egg, beaten
1 large (500 ml) can Guinness

Preheat oven to about 400°F/200°C/gas 6. Mix dry ingredients well. Blend in the liquids to make a wet dough (water will do if extra liquid is needed). Turn into a greased loaf tin. Bake in a hot oven for about 45 minutes, until well-risen, nicely browned and hollow-sounding when tapped on the base.

Cakes & Biscuits

Justifiably proud of their skills, many Irish cooks are still baking the traditional tea-time treats like Seed Cake, Rich Cherry Cake and Porter Cake — mostly for the sheer pleasure of it but also so that visitors to Ireland can share that pleasure. The recipes in this section include a few of the classics, along with favourites from around the country. Some are versatile enough to be at home on the tea table or dressed up as desserts for dinner. Sometimes the simplest really are best: what could be more delicious than a feather-light sponge cake layered as a gâteau and served with whipped cream and seasonal soft fruit? There are more informal baked goods, including some chewy biscuits, along with suggestions for savoury biscuits which are good enough to serve with Ireland's delicious farmhouse cheeses.

Cakes

Seed Cake

Caraway seeds have had a long history in Irish baking. This traditional treat has appeared on many a tea table down through the generations. It keeps well in an airtight tin. Makes 1 cake.

> 8 oz/225g/2 cups plain (all-purpose) flour
> 4 oz/100g/1 stick butter, at room temperature
> 4 oz/100g/4 US tbsp caster (superfine) sugar
> 2 large eggs, beaten
> 1 level tsp/1¼ US tsp baking powder
> 1 rounded dsp/1½ US tbsp caraway seeds
> a little milk, if required
> extra caraway seeds, for sprinkling

Preheat a moderate oven, 350°F/180°C/gas 4. Line the base of a buttered 6-7"/ 15-18 cm deep cake tin with buttered greaseproof/waxed paper.

Sift the flour. Cream the butter and sugar until light and fluffy. By degrees, add the eggs to the sugar mixture, along with a spoonful of flour with each addition. Add the baking powder and caraway seeds with the last spoonful of flour. Mix lightly but thoroughly, adding a little milk to make a soft mixture if it seems too stiff. Turn into the prepared tin and sprinkle with a few extra caraway seeds.

Bake for 15 minutes. Then reduce the temperature to 325°F/160°C/gas 3 for about 1 hour, until the cake is well-risen, golden-brown and shrinking away from the tin a little. Leave to cool in the tin for about 10 minutes. Remove and finish cooling on a wire rack. When cold, take off the baking paper and store in an airtight tin.

Variation

This can be adapted to make a traditional spice cake. Sift in 1½ tsp of mixed spices (ground cloves, cinnamon and nutmeg) with the flour and omit the caraway seeds.

Cherry Cake

This is one of my favourites. Rich and moist, it has a lovely crunchy top and a generous allocation of cherries. If given the chance, it keeps exceptionally well. Makes one 7-8"/18-20 cm cake.

> 8 oz/225g/2 cups flour
> pinch of salt
> ½ tsp baking powder
> 8 oz/225g/1½ cups glacé cherries
> 6 oz/175g/1½ stick butter
> 6 oz/175g/6 US tbsp caster (superfine) sugar
> 2 large eggs, beaten
> milk, to mix
> a few drops of vanilla essence
> 1 oz/25g/1 US tbsp granulated sugar, to sprinkle

Preheat a moderate oven, 350°F/180°C/gas 4. Grease and base-line a 7-8"/18-20 cm loose-based deep cake tin.

Sift the flour, salt and baking powder into a bowl. Quarter most of the cherries and mix them in with the flour. Halve the remaining cherries and set aside.

Cream the butter and sugar until light and fluffy. Gradually beat in the eggs, adding a little flour with each addition. Mix well. Stir in the remaining dry ingredients lightly, adding just enough milk to make to a fairly stiff mixture. Add the vanilla essence. Blend the mixture lightly but thoroughly.

Turn into the prepared tin and smooth the top. Press the reserved cherries lightly into the top of the cake and sprinkle with the granulated sugar. Bake for 1½ hours, until golden-brown and firm to the touch. Cool in the tin for 10-15 minutes, until the cake shrinks away from the tin a little. Turn out onto a wire rack and leave to cool completely. When cold, remove the baking paper and store in an airtight tin.

Irish Apple Cake

While this lovely moist cake can be made at any time, it is ideal for late autumn, when there's an abundance of apples. It seems especially well suited to Hallowe'en, although it isn't associated with Hallowe'en customs in the same way as Barm Brack. It has a lovely crunchy top and can be served cold as a cake, or warm with cream or custard as a pudding. Makes one 8"/20 cm cake.

8 oz/225g/2 cups self-raising flour
good pinch of salt
½ coffee spoon/⅛ US tsp ground cloves
4 oz/100g/1 stick butter, at room temperature
3 or 4 cooking apples (eg Armagh Bramleys)
4-6 oz/100-150g/4-6 US tbsp sugar, to taste
2 eggs, beaten
a little milk, to mix
granulated sugar, to sprinkle

Grease one 8"/20 cm cake tin. Preheat a moderately hot oven, 375°F/190°C/gas 5.

Sift the flour, salt and cloves into a bowl. Cut in the butter and rub in until the mixture is like fine breadcrumbs. Peel and core the apples. Slice thinly and add to the rubbed-in mixture. Add the sugar — the amount depends on how much sweetening the apples need. Mix in the eggs and enough milk to make a fairly stiff dough. Turn the mixture into the prepared tin and sprinkle with granulated sugar. Bake for 30-40 minutes, until crisp, golden-brown and springy to the touch.

Dried Fruit Cake

If you drop in to Sheen Falls Lodge in time for afternoon tea, that lovely waterside hotel in Kenmare, Co. Kerry, you may well be offered this delicious cake. Some of the ingredients are rather exotic — such as dried mango and pineapple — and may not be easily available. But appropriate replacements can be used as long as the balance of ingredients is the same. A lovely, moist cake, it slices well after a couple of days. Makes 2 loaf-shaped cakes.

> 8 oz/225g/2 cups wholemeal (whole-wheat) flour
> 6 oz/175g/1½ cups plain (all-purpose) flour
> 3 tsp/3¾ US tsp baking powder
> ½ tsp bread (baking) soda
> ½ tsp freshly grated nutmeg
> ½ tsp ground cloves
> ½ tsp ground mace
> 2 tsp/2½ US tsp ground cinnamon
> grated zest of 2 (washed) oranges
> 9 oz/250g/1½ cups fresh or dried dates (stoned, peeled and chopped)
> 4 oz/100g/⅔ cup Brazil nuts, chopped
> 5 oz/150g/1 cup dried pineapple, chopped
> 2 oz/50g/½ cup dried mango, chopped
> 10 oz/275g/2½ sticks butter or margarine
> 7 oz/200g/1 cup soft dark sugar
> 2 tsp/2½ US tsp grated fresh ginger
> 4 eggs
> 4 very large ripe bananas, mashed

Preheat a very moderate oven, 300°F/150°C/gas 2. Line 2 large (2 lb/900g) loaf tins with baking parchment or buttered greaseproof/waxed paper.

Combine the flours, raising agents and spices in a large bowl. In a second bowl, combine orange zest, dates, nuts and dried fruit. In a third bowl, cream the butter, sugar and fresh ginger until pale and fluffy. Then add the eggs to the butter mixture, one at a time, and beat well.

Add the flour to the butter mixture in several batches, alternating with the mashed bananas. Now fold in the fruit-nut mixture.

Divide the mixture between the 2 lined tins and flatten with a palette knife. Bake for 1-1¼ hours, until nicely browned and springy to the touch. Leave to cool in the tins. When cold, turn out of the tins but do not remove the lining papers. Wrap and store in an airtight container for 3-4 days before slicing.

Porter Cake

Porter, a weaker form of Guinness, was a key ingredient in many traditional Irish dishes, both sweet and savoury. Adding colour and richness of flavour without being over-dominant, it was known as 'single' stout. Since porter was taken off the market some years ago, Guinness has been used instead. Although it's a good substitute in recipes such as this, it is sometimes better diluted. Porter Cake remains popular all over the country. This creaming method version comes from St Ernans Country House Hotel in Donegal. Makes 1 large cake.

12 oz/350g/3 cups plain (all-purpose) flour
pinch of salt
1 tsp/1¼ US tsp baking powder
1 level tsp/1¼ US tsp mixed spice
8 oz/225g/2 sticks butter
8 oz/225g/1 cup soft dark brown sugar
3 eggs
8 oz/225g/1⅓ cups raisins
8 oz/225g/1⅓ cups sultanas (dried green grapes)
4 oz/100g/¾ cup glacé cherries
4 oz/100g/¾ cup mixed peel
2 oz/50g/½ cup almonds or walnuts, chopped
¼ pint/150 ml/½ cup Guinness (approx.)

Preheat a warm oven, 325°F/160°C/gas 3. Grease and base-line a 8"/20 cm round deep cake tin.

Sift the flour, salt, baking powder and spice into a bowl. Cream butter and brown sugar until light and fluffy. Add the eggs, one at a time, then the flour mixture. Add the fruit and nuts, then the stout. Mix well to a soft consistency.

Turn the mixture into the prepared tin and bake for 1 hour. Then reduce the heat to 300°F/150°C/gas 2 and cook for a further 1½ -2 hours, until the top is springy to the touch and a skewer thrust into the centre comes out clean. Cool in the tin, then turn out the cold cake. Remove the lining paper, wrap in fresh greaseproof/waxed paper and store in an airtight tin for at least a week before eating.

Optional

After removing the papers from the base, prick the cake all over with a skewer and spoon over a little extra stout. When it has been thoroughly absorbed, wrap the cake in greaseproof/waxed paper and store as above.

Boiled Fruit Cake

This very traditional recipe is popular throughout the country and is always a particular favourite in Belfast. It is easy to make and has an unusual texture, different from other fruit cakes This version, 'as done on the Aga' (4-oven) at Connie Aldridge's legendary country house, Mount Falcon in Co. Mayo, is even darker and more richly-flavoured than most — due to the fact that a bottle of Guinness is used instead of the usual, more prosaic '½ pint of water. . .'.

8 oz/225g/2 sticks butter or margarine
1 bottle of Guinness (½ pint/300 ml approx.)
8 oz/225g/1 cup brown sugar
1 lb/450g/2¾ cups raisins
1 lb/450g/2¾ cups sultanas (dried green grapes)
10 oz/275g/2½ cups plain (all-purpose) flour
1 tsp/1¼ US tsp baking powder
1 tsp/1¼ US tsp allspice
4 eggs
¼ pint/150 ml/½ cup milk (approx.)

Butter and base-line a deep 8"/20 cm cake tin.

Put the butter or margarine, Guinness, sugar, raisins and sultanas into a heavy-bottomed saucepan. Bring slowly up to the boil, stirring to dissolve the sugar. Boil for about 10 minutes. Then remove from the heat, turn into a mixing bowl and leave to cool until it is warm rather than hot.

Meanwhile, unless using an Aga, preheat a fairly hot oven, 375°F/190°C/gas 5.

Sift together the flour, baking powder and allspice. Beat the eggs with a little of the milk.

When the Guinness mixture has cooled enough (so that it will not curdle the eggs as they are added), slowly add in the beaten eggs and milk. Next add the flour mixture, mixing everything together with as much milk as is needed to make a stiff mixture. Turn into the prepared tin and bake in the top oven of the Aga (or the preheated oven) for about ½ hour. Then move to the lower oven of the Aga for another ½ hour (or reduce the oven to moderate, 325°F/160°C/gas 3). Finally, move the cake to the simmering oven (or turn down to cool, 275°F/140°C/gas 1) for another hour.

Keep a close eye on this when making it for the first time. Be prepared to make adjustments, especially if not using a 4-oven Aga, as it is difficult to give accurate temperatures and times for different ovens.

When ready, the cake will be springy to the touch and shrink slightly from the tin. Remove from the oven and allow to cool in the tin. Then turn out, wrap in fresh greaseproof/waxed paper and store in an airtight tin until required.

Gur Cake

A distant relative of bread-and-butter pudding (as it's a way of recycling stale bread or cake), Gur Cake is an economical, spicy fruit 'cake' which is still made and often sold in bakeries under various names such as Fruit Slice. It is often made with puff pastry, when it looks a bit like an Eccles Cake, although shortcrust pastry is more usual.

Gur Cake used to be available very cheaply from Dublin bakers. They made it with day-old bread and plain cakes (using margarine or lard rather than the butter used here). It was very popular with poor families in the last century and the first half of this one. Can also be used to recycle fruit cake or brack that is past its best, in which case the fruit should be omitted. Makes 2 dozen.

> 8 slices stale bread or equivalent cake
> 3 oz/75g/6 US tbsp plain (all-purpose) flour
> pinch of salt
> ½ tsp baking powder
> 2 tsp/2½ US tsp mixed spice
> 4 oz/100g/½ cup granulated sugar
> 6 oz/175g/1¼ cups currants or mixed dried fruit
> 2 oz/50g/½ stick butter, melted
> 1 egg, beaten
> milk, to mix
> 8 oz/225g shortcrust pastry
> caster (superfine) sugar, to sprinkle

Remove the crusts from the bread and rub the rest to make crumbs. Put the crumbs into a mixing bowl with the flour, salt, baking powder, mixed spice, sugar and dried fruit. Mix well. Melt the butter and beat the egg. Add to the dry ingredients with enough milk to make a fairly stiff, spreadable mixture.

Preheat a moderately hot oven, 375°F/190°C/gas 5.

Roll out the shortcrust pastry and, using an 11" x 7"/27.9x17.8 cm oblong baking tin as a guide, cut out a piece to make the lid. Use the rest, re-rolled as necessary, to line the base of the tin.

Spread the pastry with the fruit mixture, then cover with the pastry lid. Using a sharp knife, make diagonal slashes across the top at regular intervals. Bake for 50-60 minutes, until crisp and golden-brown. Sprinkle the top with caster (superfine) sugar and leave to cool in the tin, then cut into slices.

Irish Whiskey Cake

This is one of my favourites. With its subtle flavours of lemon and cloves, it is reminiscent of hot Irish whiskey. Makes one 7"/18 cm cake.

8 oz/225g/1⅓ cups sultanas (dried green grapes)
grated zest of l lemon
¼ pint/150 ml/½ cup Irish whiskey
6 oz/175g/1½ sticks softened butter
6 oz/175g/¾ cup soft brown sugar
3 large eggs, separated
6 oz/175g/1½ cups plain (all-purpose) flour
pinch of salt
pinch of ground cloves
l tsp/1½ tsp baking powder

Icing
juice of the lemon
8 oz/225g/1¾ cups icing (confectioners') sugar
a little warm water
crystallised lemon slices (optional)

Put the sultanas and grated lemon zest into a bowl with the whiskey. Leave to soak overnight.

Grease and base-line a 7"/18 cm deep cake tin, preferably loose-based, and preheat a moderate oven, 350°F/180°C/gas 4.

Cream the butter and sugar until light and fluffy. Separate the eggs and set aside. Sift the flour, salt, cloves and baking powder together into a bowl. Beat the yolks into the butter and sugar little by little, including a spoonful of flour and beating well after each addition. Gradually add in the sultana and whiskey mixture, alternating with the remaining flour. *Do not over-beat at this stage.* Finally, whisk the egg whites until stiff and fold them into the mixture with a metal spoon.

Turn into the prepared tin and bake for about 1½ hours, until well-risen and springy to the touch. Test with a skewer, which should come out clean, if you are uncertain. Turn out and cool on a rack.

Meanwhile, make the icing by mixing the lemon juice with the sifted icing (confectioners') sugar and just enough warm water to make a pouring consistency. Put a dinner plate under the cake rack to catch the drips and pour the icing over the cake a tablespoon at a time, letting it dribble naturally down the sides. Don't worry if a lot of it ends up on the plate underneath — just scoop it up and put it on top again. When the icing has set, decorate the cake with crystallised lemon slices, if you like.

Irish Coffee Cake

The recipe for this lovely, luscious treat was given to me by Paula Daly, one of the great bakers of this generation. Virtually single-handed, she kept people all over Ireland interested in baking through her radio programmes, books and advisory services during the dark decades when it looked as if home baking might disappear forever. This delicious cake can be used as a dessert or, like a gâteau, eaten with a fork with tea or coffee. It is made in a ring shape, which makes it much easier to serve — and leftovers are never a problem. Makes one 8"/20 cm ring cake.

> 4 oz/100g/1 stick butter, at room temperature
> 4 oz/100g/4 US tbsp caster (superfine) sugar
> 2 eggs, beaten
> 4 oz/100g/1 cup self-raising flour
> 1-2 tbsp/1¼-2½ US tbsp coffee essence

Irish coffee syrup
> ¼ pint/150 ml/½ cup strong black coffee
> 4 oz/100g/4 US tbsp granulated sugar
> 4 tbsp/5 US tbsp Irish whiskey

To decorate
> ¼ pint/150 ml/½ cup double cream
> icing (confectioners') sugar, to taste
> l tbsp whiskey, or to taste
> chopped nuts or grated chocolate

Grease and flour an 8"/20 cm ring cake tin. Preheat a moderate oven, 350°F/180°C/gas 4.

Cream the butter and sugar until light and fluffy. Beat in the eggs, adding some flour and beating well after each addition. When egg and flour are fully incorporated, stir in the coffee essence and mix thoroughly. Turn the mixture into the prepared tin and bake for 35-40 minutes, until springy to the touch. Turn out and cool on a wire rack.

To make the Irish coffee syrup, put the coffee and sugar into a small pan and bring to the boil, stirring to dissolve the sugar. Boil for l minute. Remove from the heat and add the whiskey. Wash and dry the tin in which the cake was baked and return the cooled cake to it. Then pour the hot coffee syrup all over it. Leave in a cool place for several hours, then turn out.

To decorate, whip the cream until it is thick and sweeten lightly with sifted icing (confectioners') sugar. Add whiskey to taste. Spread the cake with the whipped cream and chill for an hour before serving, sprinkled with chopped nuts or grated chocolate.

Chocolate Hazelnut Cake

This scrumptious confection, from Susan Kellett of Enniscoe House, Co. Mayo, is more of a gâteau than a cake and well suited to serving with a cake fork with coffee or as a dessert. Makes one 9"/23 cm deep cake.

8 oz/225g/2 sticks unsalted butter
8 oz/225g/1¼ cups soft brown sugar
4 eggs, separated
4 oz/100g/1 cup self-raising flour, sifted
pinch of salt
4 oz/100g/¾ cup ground hazelnuts
8 oz/225g/8 squares plain chocolate, grated

To finish
½ pint/300 ml/1¼ cups double cream
2 oz/50g/⅓ cup hazelnuts, chopped
6 oz/175g/6 squares plain chocolate
4 oz/100g/⅔ cup icing (confectioners') sugar
4 tbsp water

Grease a 9"/23 cm deep cake tin and line with baking parchment/waxed paper. Preheat a very moderate oven, 325°F/170°C/gas 3.

Beat the butter and brown sugar together until light and fluffy. Beat in the egg yolks slowly, adding a little of the sifted flour and salt with each addition. Fold in the remaining flour, then the hazelnuts and grated chocolate. Mix well.

Beat the egg whites until stiff. Fold into the cake mixture and spoon into the prepared cake tin. Level the top and bake for about 1 hour. Test with a skewer, which will come out clean when the cake is cooked. Remove from the oven and leave to cool in the tin.

When cold, turn the cake out of the tin, peel off the paper and slice the cake in half.

To finish
Whip the cream until firm. Spread over one half of the cake and sprinkle with half of the chopped nuts. Place the other half of the cake on top. Put the chocolate, icing (confectioners') sugar and water into a bowl and stand in a pan of simmering water. Heat gently until the chocolate has melted. Keep stirring with a wooden spoon. Spread this icing over the top of the cake, sprinkle the remaining nuts on top and serve as soon as possible.

Sponge Layer Gâteau

Aine Schwalm's luscious gâteau, made at the Roundwood Inn high in the Wicklow Hills, is ideal for entertaining, as it needs to be made a couple of days ahead. The recipe here is for one layer, although it can be doubled or trebled, depending on the size of gâteau wanted. It can also be made plain, chocolate, or a mixture. The sponges can be layered up simply with whipped cream and sliced strawberries or fresh raspberries to make a quick soft fruit gâteau. Makes one gâteau 10 ½ "/27 cm diameter and 1 ¼"/3 cm deep.

> 2 oz/50g/2 US tbsp cornflour (corn starch)
> 1 oz/25g/2 US tbsp plain (all-purpose) flour
> 3 small eggs, separated
> 3 oz/75g/3 US tbsp caster (superfine) sugar
> 2 dsp/2½ US tbsp warm water

Preheat a hot oven, 425°F/220°C/gas 7. Thoroughly grease a tin 10½ "/27 cm diameter and 1¼"/3 cm deep.

Sift the flours together. Separate the eggs and whisk the whites until stiff. Add the sugar and yolks to the whites and whisk until creamy and thick. Then, using a metal spoon, carefully and lightly fold the flours into the egg mixture and, lastly, the warm water.

Pour the mixture into the prepared tin and bake for 7-11 minutes, until golden-brown and springy to the touch. Leave in the tin a minute or two, then carefully turn out and cool on a wire rack. When cold, the sponge can be stored in a dry place for some time before use.

Variations

*To make a chocolate layer, sift about 2 tsp of cocoa powder in with the flours.
*Sprinkle some Baileys Irish Cream, Croft Sherry or your favourite liqueur onto the sponge — be generous, but do not soak it.
*Cover each layer with mashed bananas and/or strawberries or raspberries and leave for a few minutes to soak through. Then add fresh cream, whipped with a little sugar until stiff. The outer layer can be covered with cream and, perhaps, coated with toasted chopped nuts, if you like. Chill for at least 48 hours before use, to allow the flavours to mingle and develop.

Ballylickey Yummy Cake

What can be said about this variation on the classic fatless sponge, using ground almonds and semolina instead of flour — except that it is aptly named? Try it for yourself! George Graves of Ballylickey House, near Bantry, Co. Cork, serves it with raspberries fresh from the garden. Makes one 8"/20 cm cake.

> 3 large eggs, separated
> 4 oz/100g/4 US tbsp caster (superfine) sugar
> rind and juice of ½ lemon
> 2 oz/50g/¼ cup fine semolina
> ½ oz/15g/1 US tbsp ground almonds

To serve
¼ pint/150 ml/½ cup cream
kirsch or maraschino, to taste
8 oz/225g raspberries

Butter an 8"/20 cm cake tin. Line with buttered greaseproof/waxed paper and dust
with a mixture of equal quantities of flour and caster (superfine) sugar (about half
a tablespoon each). Tap out any excess and set aside. Preheat a moderate oven,
350°F/180°C/gas 4.

Separate the eggs. Whisk the yolks and sugar together until the mixture makes a
'ribbon' when the whisk is lifted from it. Then add the lemon juice and rind.
Whisk again until the same 'ribbon' texture is reached. Gently stir in the semolina
and ground almonds to amalgamate thoroughly without losing volume. Whisk the
egg whites until stiff but not dry and carefully fold into the mixture with a metal
spoon. Turn into the prepared tin and bake in the centre of the oven for
30-40 minutes, until just firm to the touch and shrinking slightly from the tin.
Cool on a wire rack, removing the baking paper when cool enough to handle.

To serve, whip the cream and flavour with a little kirsch or maraschino. Split the
cake, sandwich with whipped cream and top with the raspberries, which may be
dusted with a little icing (confectioners') sugar. Serve as a cake or as a pudding.

Carrot Cake

This is usually tagged with a 'health food' image — and the recipe is most often
American. Not so this very different recipe from Rathmullan House, on the shores
of Lough Swilly in Co. Donegal. This is more like an Austrian carrot cake, rich with
almonds and lots of creamy eggs. Makes one 10-11"/26-29 cm cake.

6 eggs, separated
zest of 2 lemons
11 oz/300g/1⅔ cups caster (superfine) sugar
11 oz/300g/2 cups ground almonds
3 oz/75g/3 US tbsp cornflour (corn starch)
good pinch of cinnamon
¼ oz/7g/1 ¼ US tsp baking powder
11 oz/300g/2 cups grated carrots

Preheat a moderate oven, 350°F/180°C/gas 4. Butter a deep loose-based or spring-
form 10-11"/26-29 cm cake tin.

Separate the eggs. wash and dry the lemons and grate the zest finely. Beat the
sugar, egg yolks and lemon zest until very pale and creamy. Add the almonds,
cornflour, cinnamon, baking powder and carrots and mix thoroughly. Whisk the
egg whites until stiff and fold into the mixture. Turn into the buttered tin and
bake for about 1 hour, until springy to the touch and shrinking slightly from the
tin.Leave to cool in the tin for 10 minutes before turning out onto a rack. Keep
for 2 or 3 days, if possible, before cutting. Dredge with icing (confectioners')
sugar to serve.

Crunchy Date Cake

This more-ish cake is just the thing to have with afternoon tea or morning coffee to boost energy levels. The crunchy oat flakes contrast nicely with the moistness in the middle — and the stout in the filling enriches the flavour, giving it an unusual tang. Makes one oblong cake, 10"/25 cm x 8"/20 cm.

> 6 oz/175g/1½ cups self-raising flour
> 4 oz/100g/⅔ cup oat flakes
> good pinch of salt
> 6 oz/175g/scant 1 cup soft brown sugar
> 5 oz/150g/1¼ sticks butter or margarine, melted

Filling
6 oz/175g/1½ cups self-raising flour
12 oz/350g/1¾ cups pressed dates, chopped
6 fl oz/175 ml/¾ cup stout (Guinness, Beamish or Murphy's)

First prepare the filling. Put the chopped dates into a saucepan with the Guinness. Bring to the boil and simmer, stirring constantly, until thick and jammy. Set aside.

Preheat a fairly hot oven, 375°F/190°C/gas 5. Thoroughly grease an oblong baking tin, 10"/25 cm x 8"/20 cm.

Mix together the flour, oat flakes, salt and brown sugar. Melt the butter or margarine and stir it into the mixture. Turn half of it into the prepared tin, spread out and flatten it down with a palette knife. Then cover with the date mixture. Spread evenly, then cover with the remaining oat mixture. Spread out and smooth down with a palette knife. Bake for about 1 hour, until crisp and golden-brown. Then slide a knife around the edge to loosen from the tin, turn out carefully and cool on a wire rack. When cold, cut into squares or fingers to serve.

Variation

Water sharpened with a little lemon juice can be used to replace the Guinness. Some grated lemon zest included in the mixture is good too.

BISCUITS (including plain biscuits for cheese)

Glassdrumman Flapjacks

These are a tea-time treat at Graeme and Joan Hall's Glassdrumman Lodge in the foothills of the Mourne Mountains near Annalong, Co. Down. They may 'grow the stones for stone walls' around here, but there's a softer side to its nature too, as chef Stephen Webb demonstrates with the good things he enjoys baking for guests. These flapjacks are hard to categorise, being too crisp for a cake and rather chewy to be a biscuit — but they are closer to the biscuit. Makes about 2 dozen.

> 3 oz/75g/¾ stick butter
> 3 oz/75g/3 US tbsp sugar
> 1 dsp/1½ US tbsp golden (Karo) syrup
> 1 dsp/1½ US tbsp honey
> 4 oz/100g/⅔ cup folled oats

Preheat a fairly hot oven, 375°F/190°C/gas 5.

In a saucepan, mix all the ingredients except the oats, stirring until everything is dissolved. Add the oats and stir in. Turn the mixture into a greased shallow baking tin (Swiss roll/jelly roll tin). Spread out evenly and press down well with a flat-bottomed glass. Bake for about 10-15 minutes, until browned but not hard. Remove from the oven and cut into squares while warm. Leave to cool on a wire rack. Keeps well in an airtight tin.

Wheaten Biscuits

Elizabeth Hegarty runs an exceptional farmhouse 'country guesthouse' at Greenhill House, near Coleraine. Her guests are invariably treated to a wonderful spread of the irresistible home baking for which Northern Ireland is rightly famous. Elizabeth is generous with her recipes, which include these crisp little delights. Despite the name, they are made with oat flakes and taste of coconut! Makes about 3 dozen.

> 8 oz/225g/2 sticks margarine
> 4 oz/100g/½ cup caster (superfine) sugar
> 4 oz/100g/1 cup self-raising flour
> 2 oz/50g/⅔ cup desiccated coconut
> 8 oz/225g/1⅓ cups oat flakes

Preheat a moderate oven, 350°F/180°C/gas 4.

Cream margarine and sugar together. Add flour, coconut and oat flakes. Mix well. Roll out and cut into small rounds and arrange on lightly greased baking trays. Bake until golden-brown, about 15-20 minutes.

Ginger Biscuits

Hazel Bourke's crisp, crunchy biscuits are served with afternoon tea or morning coffee at the wonderfully hospitable Assolas House, near Kanturk in Co. Cork. Makes about 40.

> 4 oz/100g/1 stick butter
> 8 oz/225g/1 cup caster (superfine) sugar
> 1 egg
> 1 tsp/1¼ US tsp golden (Karo) syrup
> 8 oz/225g/2 cups flour
> ½ tsp baking powder
> 2 level tsp/2½ US tsp ground ginger

Preheat a moderate oven, 350°F/180°C/gas 4.

Cream the butter and sugar well until pale and fluffy. Beat in the egg and add the syrup. Mix well. Sift dry ingredients together, then sift into the egg mixture. Mix thoroughly to form a stiff dough. Shape into small balls the size of a walnut and arrange on greased baking sheets, spacing well apart to allow for spreading during cooking. Bake until golden-brown, about 15 minutes. Allow to cool a little on the trays, then lift carefully onto wire racks. When cold, store in an airtight tin.

Rich Chocolate Cookies

These come from Myrtle Allen's famous farmhouse kitchen at Ballymaloe House, Co. Cork. Mrs Allen points out that there is no need to grease the baking sheets for these biscuits as they have a high fat content — and, if cooking chocolate is used, the butter can be slightly reduced. This recipe makes flat, crisp biscuits which are delicious served with coffee. Makes about 20.

> 3½ oz/90g/3-4 squares plain chocolate, grated
> 4 oz/100g/1 stick butter
> 4 oz/100g/4 US tbsp caster (superfine) sugar
> 4 oz/100g/1 cup plain (all-purpose) flour
> ½ oz/15g/1 US tsp almonds (or other nuts), chopped

Preheat a moderate oven, 350°F/180°C/gas 4.

Grate the chocolate and beat with the butter, caster (superfine) sugar and flour until smooth. Add the chopped nuts. Dot teaspoonsful of this mixture onto baking sheets, allowing plenty of room for them to spread. Bake until well browned, about 15-20 minutes. Leave on the baking tray for a few minutes before transferring to a wire rack to cool. Store in an airtight tin.

Shortbread Fingers

At Doyle's seafood restaurant in Dingle, Stella Doyle makes these to serve with residents' coffee or to accompany desserts. It's an easy all-in-one recipe which makes very light, crisp shortbread with an excellent flavour. Keeps well. Makes about 48 fingers.

10 oz/275g/2½ cups plain (all-purpose) flour
1 oz/25g/1 US tbsp ground almonds
8 oz/225g/2 sticks soft butter
3 oz/75g/3 US tbsp caster (superfine) sugar
grated rind of ½ lemon

Preheat a moderate oven, 350°F/180°C/gas 4. Oil a fairly big baking tray or Swiss roll/jelly roll tin.

Put all ingredients into a mixer or food processor and beat until the mixture comes together. Put onto the oiled tray in lumps and flatten out until even all over. Bake for about 20 minutes, until pale golden-brown. Take out of the oven and mark into fingers or squares at once. Allow to cool a little, then transfer to a wire rack and leave until cold. Store in an airtight box.

Biscuits for Cheese

Plain Oatmeal Biscuits

These are delicious with plenty of butter and any cheese, forming the ideal partnership on the cheese board. They're not hard to make as long as you don't expect them to turn out as neatly as bought ones. Makes about 18.

3 oz/75g/6 US tbsp plain (all-purpose) flour
½ tsp salt
¼ tsp baking powder
4 oz/100g/2/3 cup fine medium oatmeal
2½ oz/65g/1½ US tbsp dripping or white fat (lard)
cold water, to mix

Preheated a moderately hot oven, 400°F/200°C/gas 6.

Sift together the flour, salt and baking powder. Add oatmeal and mix well. Rub in fat until crumbly, then mix with just enough cold water to make a stiff dough. Turn onto a worktop sprinkled with fine oatmeal and knead until smooth and manageable. Roll out thinly (⅛"/0.3 cm) and cut into rounds, squares or triangles. Bake for about 15 minutes, until crisp. Cool on a wire rack and store in an airtight tin, preferably lined with greaseproof paper, when absolutely cold. Check for crispness before serving. Reheat briefly to crisp, if necessary.

(For traditional oatcakes cooked on the griddle, see 'Hot off the Griddle'.)

Enniscoe Oatmeal Biscuits with Curry Powder

Enniscoe, 'the last great house of North Mayo', was built by Susan Kellett's ancestors in the 1660s. Susan now runs it as an hospitable country house and genealogy centre. Good home-cooking at dinner includes home-made biscuits to serve with cheese. The next two recipes are among her favourites. Makes about 24.

> 5 oz/150g/1¼ cups wholemeal (whole-wheat) flour
> 3 oz/75g/¾ US tbsp medium oatmeal
> 4 tsp/5 US tsp brown sugar
> 1 tsp/1¼ US tsp baking powder
> ½ tsp salt
> ½ tsp curry powder
> 4 oz/100g/1 stick butter
> a little milk, to mix

Preheat a moderate oven, 350°F/180°C/gas 4.

In a mixing bowl, combine the dry ingredients thoroughly. Then rub in the butter to make a mixture like fine breadcrumbs. Add enough milk to make a slightly wet dough. Turn onto a floured board and roll out thinly, about 1⅛"/0.3 cm thick. Cut into rounds. (If necessary, more milk can be added to make the dough workable when re-rolling the trimmings.) Using a palette knife, lift the biscuits onto greased baking sheets. Bake for about 20 minutes, until firm and lightly browned. Leave to cool on the baking tray for about 5 minutes before transferring to a wire rack. Store in an airtight tin when completely cold.

Wholemeal Biscuits

These are also from Enniscoe and are rather like unsweetened digestive biscuits. Makes about 30.

> 5 oz/150g/1 heaped cup fine wholemeal (whole-wheat) flour
> 3 oz/75g/6 US tbsp plain (all-purpose) flour
> ½ tsp baking powder
> ½ tsp salt
> 2 oz/50g/½ stick butter
> water, to mix

Preheat a very moderate oven, 300°F/150°C/gas 2.

Combine the dry ingredients in a mixing bowl. Rub in the butter and mix in enough water to make a firm dough. Turn onto a floured board and roll out very thinly and cut into rounds. Bake for about 30 minutes, until crisp and lightly browned. Cool on a wire rack and store in an airtight tin when cold.

Water Biscuits

These are made for serving with cheese at the King Sitric, the seafood restaurant on the harbour-front in Howth, Co. Dublin. If the biscuits are pricked with a fork before baking, they will be flat; otherwise they will puff up unevenly to become the attractive little biscuits known as 'Blisters'. Either way, they're an asset to any cheese board. Makes about 1 dozen.

> 4 oz/100g/1 cup self-raising flour
> pinch of salt
> 2 tbsp/2½ US tbsp water
> ½ oz/15g/1 US tbsp butter or margarine, melted

Preheat a moderately hot oven, 400°F/200°C/gas 6.

Sift flour and salt into a basin. Heat fat in water to melt. Pour into the flour and mix to a smooth paste. Turn onto a floured board and knead until smooth and manageable. Roll out thinly and stamp into small rounds or cut into squares. Bake for 15-20 minutes, until golden-brown on both sides. Cool on a rack, toss in salt and, when absolutely cold, store in an airtight tin.

Pastry & Puddings

'So if you're down in Dingle and you think starvation's near
Just take a walk along Strand Road til you come down to the pier.
Tis there you'll find de Barra's, you'll know just where it lies
When your nostrils know they're on the scent of Maire's Mutton Pies.'
From The Mutton Pie Song, *by Paul Creighton*

A light hand with pastry and 'a nice dessert' on the dinner table have always
been points of pride for Irish cooks. The recipes in this chapter give a fair
cross-section of the style of pastry dishes and puddings that are being made today,
whether of historical interest — such as Dingle Pies — or simply because they are
both tasty and popular.

The best traditional Irish puddings are comforting dishes based on those
ingredients, both cultivated and wild, which do well in the Irish climate, such as
rhubarb and gooseberries, apples and pears, bilberries ('fraughan') and blackberries.
Nuts such as walnuts, hazelnuts and almonds have always been enjoyed. Walnuts
were quite common until the nineteenth century when they virtually disappeared
because the wood was in demand to make gun stocks. Hazelnuts are still easily found,
although they are not harvested commercially; almonds, a favourite ingredient since
the eighteenth century, have always been imported.

Honey has been used as a natural sweetener since earliest times. Although sugar
has also been in use for hundreds of years now and is an important agricultural
crop, many dishes depend on honey for its unique texture and flavour — not to
mention any special healthy qualities it may have.

Another major ingredient in Ireland has always been milk, the basis for many
traditional baked puddings made with oatmeal, barley or, from the mid-nineteenth
century, rice. As cream would generally have been used to make butter, leaving the
skimmed milk for cooking, richer dishes using cream tend to be modern, or else of
the 'country house cooking' style, typical of finer fare in the 'big houses'.

Note to American readers

In Ireland, 'pudding' may refer to either a sweet or savoury dish. The word may also
refer to the dessert course or to a type of meat sausage called black or white pudding.
(See Chapter 6 and Chapter 9 for more dessert and cake recipes.)

Dingle Pies

At Mhaire de Barra's Dingle pub, they make the real thing, traditional meat pies. Not unlike Cornish pasties, they are traditional in the Dingle area for special occasions such as Lammas Day, and at Puck Fair in nearby Killorglin. There are numerous recipes for mutton pies in the Dingle area. The pastry used to be shortened with dripping or mutton fat, as in the authentic all-meat pies made by Eileen McCarthy at Mhaire de Barra's. With crusts more like a white bread dough (without the soda), they were either served straight from the oven, or cooled and then boiled in mutton stock (which not only moistens but also makes them bigger and softer). Now, shortcrust pastry made with butter or a mixture of butter and white fats is more often used, as in this modern variation which, unlike older recipes, also contains vegetables. Makes 6 pies.

Pastry
1 lb 2 oz/500g/4½ cups plain (all-purpose) flour
9 oz/250g/2¼ sticks butter (or ½ butter and ½ white fat)
4 fl oz/100 ml/scant ½ ½ cup very cold water

Sift the flour into a large bowl. Cut the fat into small pieces and add to the flour. Rub in with finger tips or pastry blender, lifting the mixture as much as possible to aerate. Add the chilled water. Mix with a knife or fork until the mixture clings together. Turn onto a floured worktop and knead lightly once or twice until smooth. Wrap in clingfilm/foil and leave in the fridge to relax for 20 minutes before using.

Filling
1 lb/450g boneless mutton or lamb
1 large onion
2 carrots
1 potato
2 sticks of celery
salt and pepper
1 egg, beaten, to brush

Preheat a moderate oven, 350°F/180°C/gas 4.

Trim any fat or gristle from the meat and cut it up very small. Peel the onion, carrots and potato and cut into small dice. Trim the celery and cut into similar dice. Mix the meat and vegetables together and season with salt and pepper.

Cut ⅓ off the ball of pastry and reserve to make lids for the pies. Roll out the rest and, using a small plate as a guide and re-rolling the pastry as necessary, cut out 6 circles.

Divide the meat and vegetable mixture between the six, piling it neatly in the middle of each. Roll out the remaining pastry and cut out six smaller circles. Lay these on top of the piles of meat. Dampen the edges of the pastry bases, bring the pastry up around the meat and pleat it to fit the lid. Pinch the two edges together. Make a little hole in the top of each pie to let out the steam. Brush tops with beaten egg and slide the pies onto baking sheets. Bake for 1 hour.

Eat hot or cold — the original pies used to make a handy portable meal for farmers and fishermen, so they're ideal for picnics. If you happen to have lamb gravy left over from a roast, mix a little in with the raw ingredients to make the pies juicier.

Steak & Oyster Pie

Although impervious to the whims of food fashion at Ballymaloe House in Co. Cork, their old-fashioned pie is a good example of the kind of food which is coming back into vogue at smart restaurants. It's never been out of style at Ballymaloe, of course. Serves 6-8.

    3 tbsp/3-4 US tbsp unsalted butter
    1½ lb/700g boneless beef, cut into cubes
    1 large onion, chopped
    1 tbsp/1¼ US tbsp flour
    1 pint /600 ml/2½ cups beef stock or canned beef broth
    12 oysters, shucked, reserving liquor
    salt
    freshly ground black pepper
    6 oz/175g/2 cups sliced mushrooms
    12 oz/350g puff pastry, home-made or bought, thawed if frozen

Heat 2 tbsp of the butter in a heavy flame-proof casserole and brown the beef in it, in batches, over medium heat. Do not crowd the meat and watch carefully so that the butter does not burn. Add the onion and cook for 2-3 minutes. Stir in the flour and cook, stirring, for 2 minutes. Add the beef stock, the oysters, the reserved oyster liquor and the salt (omit salt if using canned beef broth) and pepper. Bring the mixture just to a boil. Cover. Bake the mixture in a preheated oven, 180°C/350°F/gas 4, for about 1 hour, or until the meat is tender.

Meanwhile, sauté the mushrooms in the remaining butter for about 2 minutes, until softened. When the meat is tender, remove from the oven and stir in the mushrooms.

Transfer to a 4-pint/2.4 litre shallow baking dish. Raise oven temperature to 230°C/450°F/gas 8.

On a lightly floured surface, roll out the pastry to ⅛"-¼"/0.3-0.6 cm thick and drape it over the mixture in the baking dish, leaving a 1" overhang. Crimp the edges decoratively and cut a steam vent in the top of the pastry with a sharp knife.

Bake in the centre of the oven for 5 minutes. Then lower the heat to 220°C/425°F/gas 7 and bake for 15-20 minutes more, until the filling is bubbling and the pastry is golden-brown and flaky. Serve immediately.

Beefsteak & Kidney Pie with Suet Crust

This classic recipe, an excellent way of stretching a modest amount of meat, has stood the test of time. As a family meal it's unbeatable and can be a great home-made 'convenience' food — for years, when there were a lot of mouths to feed, 'Saturday Pie' saved the day at busy weekends. The filling was made ahead in an electric slow cooker, then a couple of pies were made up and frozen, ready to go straight into the oven. If you've never had a home-made steak and kidney pie with a real suet crust, don't be put off by the mass-produced variety, which is only a pale imitation of the real thing. Try this and give yourself a treat. Serves 4-6.

Filling

1½ lb/700g rib steak
l tbsp/1¼ US tbsp plain (all-purpose) flour, seasoned
½ lb/225g beef kidney or 2-3 lambs' kidneys
2 onions
l clove garlic
4 oz/100g mushrooms
2 tbsp/2½ US tbsp dripping or oil
¾ pint/450 ml/2 cups water
l tbsp/1¼ US tbsp tomato purée (optional)
l tbsp/1¼ US tbsp Worcestershire sauce
½ tsp dried mixed herbs
salt
freshly ground pepper

Suet crust

4 oz/100g/1 cup self-raising flour
2 oz/50g/4 US tbsp shredded suet
salt
pepper
water, to mix
egg or milk, to brush

Remove any bones from the rib steak. Trim and chop it into bite-sized pieces. Season the flour and toss the steak in it.

Remove the skin and core from the kidney, then chop it. Peel and chop the onions, peel and crush the garlic, wipe and halve the mushrooms.

Heat the dripping or oil in a large pan and brown the steak in it, a few pieces at a time. As it browns, transfer the steak to a separate plate. Add the kidney, onion and garlic to the pan and cook for a few minutes. Then add the mushrooms. Mix the water, purée, Worcestershire sauce and herbs together and pour into the pan. Return the steak to the cooking pan, stir well and season. Cover the pan and simmer for about 1½ hours, until the meat is tender. (Or transfer to a slow cooker and cook on HIGH for 3-4 hours or on LOW overnight.)

When the meat is cooked, pour the contents of the pan into a 2 pint/l litre pie dish and allow to cool. Preheat the oven to 400°F/200°C/gas 6.

Make the suet crust. Lightly mix dry ingredients and the suet with a fork. Then add enough cold water to make a smooth, elastic dough. Leave for 5 minutes, then roll out to make a piece about 1"/2.5 cm bigger all round than the top of the pie dish. Cut off this excess strip, dampen the edge of the pie dish and press the pastry strip onto it. Then dampen the top of the strip and lay the pastry lid on top, pressing it down and sealing around the edge. Flute the edges and make a small steam hole in the centre. Decorate with any leftovers made into pastry leaves. Brush the pastry with a little beaten egg or milk and bake until the pastry is golden-brown.

Spinach & Cheese Flan

A double-crust savoury pie from Enniscree Lodge, a small hotel and restaurant in Co. Wicklow's lovely Glencree valley. It's delicious and versatile, equally useful for a starter, a snack or a vegetarian main course. As there is no need to pre-bake the pastry base, it is also simple to make. Serves 12 average portions, or 16 starters.

Pastry
1 lb 12 oz/800g/7 cups plain (all-purpose) flour
1 lb/450g/4 sticks butter
4 egg yolks
a little ice cold water, if required
egg yolk, to glaze

In a food processor, blend flour and butter until they are like fine breadcrumbs. Blend in the egg yolks and, if necessary, a little ice cold water to make a dough. When the mixture forms a ball around the knife, stop the machine and remove the dough. Knead lightly on a floured surface to make a smooth ball. Wrap in clingfilm and chill in the fridge while making the filling.

Filling
2 lb/900g spinach
a little butter and oil, for cooking
1 clove garlic, crushed, or to taste
1 lb/450g melting cheese, grated (Gabriel, Doolin or Emmenthal)
3 eggs, lightly beaten
5 fl oz/150 ml/generous ½ cup double cream
grated nutmeg
salt
freshly ground black pepper
egg yolk and salt, to glaze

Prepare the spinach. Sort, trim, wash well and shake dry. Warm a little butter and oil in a large pan, along with the garlic. Toss the spinach in it and cook gently, *without added water*, until softened and losing volume. Then stir in the grated cheese. Lightly beat the eggs and stir in with the cream, grated nutmeg to taste, a little salt (depending on how salty the cheese is) and a good grinding of black pepper.
   Preheat a moderate oven, 350°F/180°C/gas 4.
   Take the pastry from the fridge and roll out a bit more than half of it to line a 10"/25 cm spring-form tart tin. Pour the filling into the lined flan tin and roll out the remaining pastry. Dampen the edges of the pastry base, lay the pastry lid on top of the pie and trim roughly. Pinch the edges together between thumb and fore-finger to seal. Glaze by brushing with egg yolk and a light sprinkling of salt. Bake for about 40 minutes, until crisp and golden.

For flavour and texture – Walnut Bread from the Mustard Seed at Echo Lodge (page 61)

Opposite: The title tells the tale – Ballylickey Yummy Cake (page 74)

Previous page: Distinctly Mediterranean – Rathsallagh Tomato & Cheese Bread (page 55)

Enniscoe Oatmeal Biscuits with Curry Powder (page 80)

Opposite: Chocolate Hazelnut Cake, a scrumptious confection from
Enniscoe House (page 73)

Rhubarb & Cinnamon Tart – a springtime treat at Cashel House Hotel (page 88)

Perfect with coffee
or desserts – Doyle's
Shortbread Fingers
(page 79)

Opposite: Porter
Cake, an all-time
favourite at
St Ernans Country
House Hotel
(page 68)

The perfect way to round off a meal – Lemon Brûleé in an Almond Tart from Rosleague Manor (page 91)

Asparagus & Cashew Strudel with Port Wine Sauce

It is characteristic of the thoughtfully hospitable McEvilly family that they consider the special needs of their guests at Cashel House, their lovely hotel and restaurant with its own little cove and wonderful gardens in Connemara. They always have an unusual vegetarian choice on the dinner menu — this would be a typically delicious offering and is often part of their Christmas fare. Cashel was one of the first country houses to specialise in restful away-from-it-all Christmas breaks, and a special dish such as this is ideal for guests who may not enjoy the traditional turkey dinner. Serves 2 as a main course.

    1 tbsp/1¼ US tbsp olive oil
    1 onion, chopped
    1 clove garlic, crushed
    4 ripe tomatoes, skinned and chopped
    2 tsp/2½ US tsp basil, freshly chopped (when available) or 1 tsp if dried
    4 oz/100g/1¼ cup button mushrooms, washed and sliced
    4 oz/100g fresh asparagus, washed and sliced
    4 oz/100g/⅔ cup cashew nuts
    salt
    freshly ground black pepper
    10 oz/275g packet filo pastry
    4 oz/100g/1 stick butter, melted

Heat the olive oil in a large pan. Add the onions. Cover and cook gently, without colouring, until tender. Add the garlic, tomatoes and basil. Simmer gently for about 20 minutes, stirring from time to time. Add the remaining vegetables and continue to cook until tender. Then remove from the heat and adjust seasoning to taste. Leave to cool. Add the cashews when the mixture is cold. Season.

Preheat a fairly hot oven, 400°F/200°C/gas 6.

Lay a sheet of filo pastry out on a large baking sheet. Brush with melted butter, then lay another sheet of pastry on top and brush with butter. Repeat with 2 more layers of filo pastry. (Wrap up any remaining pastry and return to freezer.)

Tip the cold tomato filling mixture on top and spread it out to about 1"/2.5 cm from the edges. Fold edges in to enclose the mixture. Bake for 30 minutes and serve with Port Wine Sauce.

Port Wine Sauce
    1 tbsp/1¼ US tbsp olive oil
    1 onion, chopped
    1 clove garlic, crushed
    4 ripe tomatoes, skinned and chopped
    1 tsp fresh basil
    3 fl oz/75 ml/3 US tbsp port or red wine

Heat the oil and add the onion. Cook gently, without browning, until tender. Add the garlic, the tomatoes (together with their juices), the basil and the wine. Let the mixture simmer gently without a lid for 20 minutes. Then remove from the heat, season and serve with the strudel.

Rhubarb & Cinnamon Tart

At Cashel House, they take pride in producing as much as possible for their own table. Rhubarb flourishes mightily, so this delicious tart is often on the menu. The subtle background of almonds in the pastry and the tang of orange zest in the filling complement each other delectably, but ease of preparation is an equally powerful attraction, as the pastry case is not pre-baked. Serves 6-8.

Pastry
8 oz/225g/2 cups plain (all-purpose) flour
5 oz/150g/1¼ sticks butter
2 oz/50g/¼ cup ground almonds
2 oz/50g/2 US tbsp caster (superfine) sugar
1 egg

Filling
3 lb/1.4 kg rhubarb
4 oz/100g/4 US tbsp caster (superfine) sugar
4 level tbsp/5 US tbsp flour
1 level tsp ground cinnamon
½ pint/300 ml/1¼ cups cream
zest of 2 oranges
1 egg

First make the pastry. Sift the flour into a mixing bowl or food processor. Cut in the butter and rub in or process to make a mixture like fine breadcrumbs. Blend in the ground almonds and sugar. Add the egg and mix to make a firm dough. Roll out and use to line a 9"/23 cm flan ring (set on a baking sheet). Trim the edges and chill for half an hour.

Meanwhile, wash and chop the rhubarb.

Preheat a fairly hot oven, 375°F/190°C/gas 5.

To make the filling, combine the sugar, flour, cinnamon, cream, orange zest and egg. Blend in a food processor or beat well to make a smooth batter. Fill the pastry with the prepared rhubarb, then pour over the filling batter, coating the fruit evenly. Bake for about 50 minutes, until the fruit is tender and the top is set and golden-brown. Serve warm, dusted with icing (confectioners') sugar and accompanied by whipped cream

Rhubarb & Crab-apple Crumble

Down in Tipperary, Americans Christine and Herb Quigley run the hospitable Ballycormac House which, apart from the warmth of the welcome, is well-known for country holidays (especially anything to do with horses) and their unusual residential bread-making and baking courses that they run each year during the dark months of late winter and early spring. This scrumptious crumble is typical of the simple delights cooked for guests. It's lovely and spicy and the topping — not flour, nor even oatmeal but breadcrumbs — is unusually light. American cups are about the size of an average coffee mug. Serves 6.

1 cup each fresh white and whole-wheat breadcrumbs
1 cup brown sugar
¾ tsp ground cinnamon
¼ tsp ground cloves
¼ tsp ground nutmeg
4 tbsp melted butter
1 lb/450g rhubarb
8 crab-apples
zest and juice of ½ orange

Preheat a moderate oven, 350°F/180°C/gas 4.

Combine the breadcrumbs in a large bowl. In a small bowl, combine the sugar, cinnamon, cloves and nutmeg. Mix 2 tbsp of the spice mixture with the crumbs and add the melted butter.

Cut the rhubarb into 1" pieces. Peel and core the apples, then slice thinly. Combine the rhubarb and apples with the remaining spice mixture, the orange zest and juice. Butter a glass or ceramic casserole and spread ¾ cup of the breadcrumb mixture over the bottom. Pour in the rhubarb mixture and cover with the remaining crumbs. Cook for 45 minutes, until brown and bubbly.

Alternatively, bake in individual dishes for about 25 minutes. At Ballycormac, they partner this crumble with home-made cinnamon ice cream.

Rhubarb Soufflé Tart

Rhubarb features at the superb Beginish Restaurant in Dingle, Co. Kerry. Pat Moore's very different rhubarb tart is a delectable hot pudding. It's a real treat — and much lighter than it sounds. Makes 6 individual servings.

Pâte Sucrée
8 oz/225g/2 cups plain (all-purpose) flour
5 oz/150g /1¼ sticks butter
2 oz/50g/2 US tbsp caster (superfine) sugar
1 egg

Filling
2 bundles of rhubarb (about 2 lb/900g trimmed weight)
granulated sugar, to taste
1 egg white
caster (superfine) sugar, to sprinkle
whipped cream or Crème Anglaise (egg custard), to serve

First make the pastry. Sift the flour and put into a food processor with the butter. Process to crumb stage. Add the sugar and egg and process to make a dough. When the mixture forms a ball around the knife, turn it out onto a lightly floured worktop. Knead lightly into shape, then wrap in clingfilm and leave it in the fridge to rest for 30 minutes.

Preheat a fairly hot oven, 400°F/200°C/gas 6.

Roll out the chilled pastry to ¼" thickness and use to line six individual (4"/10 cm) tartlet tins. Line with tinfoil, weighed down with baking beans, and bake blind for 12-15 minutes. Then remove the beans and foil and return to the oven for 4-5 minutes to dry out the bases.

To make the filling

Trim the rhubarb stalks and wash them well. Cut them up and put into a saucepan, with granulated sugar to taste and just enough water to start the juices flowing. Cook gently until the fruit is tender, then leave to cool.

Whisk the egg white stiffly, then fold it into the stewed rhubarb. Fill the pastry cases with this mixture. Sprinkle the tops with caster (superfine) sugar and brown under the grill. Serve immediately with Crème Anglaise or whipped cream.

Variation

This recipe also works well with apples such as Bramley's Seedling which 'fall' during cooking to make a purée.

Frangipane Tart

This recipe was given to me by Paul Drum of Newbay House, Co. Wexford. It's one of the all-time great baked desserts — try it once and you'll be hooked. Serves 6-8.

> 1 packet (13 oz/375g) puff pastry, or equivalent home-made
> good ½ lb/225g apricot jam
> 4 large eating apples or pears (or a medium tin of pears — 8 halves)

Frangipane

> 4 oz/100g/1 stick butter, softened
> 4 oz/100g/4 US tbsp caster (superfine) sugar
> 2 eggs
> a few drops of almond essence, to taste
> 4 oz/100g-125g/⅔ cup ground almonds

Preheat a hot oven, 425°F/220°C/gas 7.

First, prepare the frangipane. Cream the butter and sugar in a food processor until light and fluffy. Add the eggs and almond essence and, finally, the ground almonds. The mixture should be quite sloppy.

Roll out the pastry once to line a 9-10"/23-25 cm loose-based tart tin, or equivalent oblong Swiss roll/jelly roll tin. Trim excess pastry and set aside.

Spread the pastry base generously with apricot jam. Peel, core and slice the apples or fresh pears. Arrange fruit on top of the jam. Pour the frangipane mixture over to coat the fruit evenly, then use up any pastry trimmings to make up a rough trellis pattern on top — it doesn't need to be very precise.

Bake in the centre of the oven, keeping an eye on it to prevent over-browning. The temperature can be reduced to 375°F/190°C/gas 5 once the pastry has browned and the filling has risen up to make a gentle golden-brown dome.

Continue baking until the pastry is crisp and the frangipane (which will sink slightly when removed from the oven) is firm and slightly springy to the touch, 45 minutes - 1 hour in all.

Serve warm, dredged with icing (confectioners') sugar and accompanied by chilled whipped cream.

Brown Bread Ice Cream

While obviously not baked, a good recipe for brown bread ice cream is ideal for
using up leftover bread. This is a particularly good version, foolproof no-stir, as
made by Phil McAfee at Restaurant St John's in Co. Donegal. The secret of its
excellent nutty flavour is to toast the bread in the oven before blending it into
crunchy crumbs — and the dash of sherry does no harm to the flavour either.

> 6 oz/175g wheaten (whole-meal) bread, toasted
> ½ pint/300 ml/1 ¼ cups double cream
> ¼ pint/150 ml/generous ½ cup single cream
> 4 oz/100g/4 US tbsp granulated sugar
> 2 eggs, separated
> 1 tsp/1¼ US tsp vanilla essence
> 2 tbsp/2½ US tbsp sweet sherry

Blend the toasted bread to make crumbs. Whisk together both creams with the
sugar, egg yolks, vanilla essence and sherry until thick. Fold in the crumbs.

Beat the egg whites in a separate bowl and fold gently into the cream mixture.
Turn into a lidded container and freeze.

Remove from the freezer 15 minutes before serving.

Lemon Brûlée in an Almond Tart

Rosleague Manor is a gracious pink-washed country house in lovely gardens,
overlooking the water at Letterfrack in Connemara. This recipe, given to me by
chef Nigel Rush, is as fine a way to round off a meal as can be imagined. The pastry
is not only very light and crisp but has a good 'kick' in it too, thanks to the rum —
and the 'burnt' filling is simply delicious. Makes an 8-9"/20-23 tart, serving 8-10.

Almond Pastry
9 oz/250g/2¼ cups plain (all-purpose) flour
7 oz/190g/1¾ sticks butter, chilled and cubed
6 oz/150g/6 US tbsp caster (superfine) sugar
2 oz/50g/⅓ cup ground almonds
1 egg yolk
1 whole egg (size 4)
finely grated rind of 1 lemon
2 generous tbsp/40 ml/2½ US tbsp dark rum

Put all pastry ingredients into a food processor and process at maximum speed
until the mixture forms a ball. Wrap in clingfilm and chill for 1 hour. Then
remove from the fridge and leave for 20 minutes.

Meanwhile, select a deep 8-9"/20-23 cm flan ring or loose-based tin and brush
the sides with oil and dust with flour. Roll the pastry out to line the tin. Trim and
set aside while making the filling.

Lemon Filling
5 small eggs (size 4)
7 oz/200g/1 cup caster (superfine) sugar
juice of 2 lemons
5 fl oz/150 ml/generous 1 cup whipping cream
icing (confectioners') sugar, to finish

First, preheat a fairly hot oven, 400°F/200°C/gas 6.
   Whisk the eggs and sugar until frothy and the sugar has dissolved into the egg. Add the lemon juice. Whip the cream lightly and fold in. Pour this mixture into the pastry case and bake for 20-25 minutes. Then sprinkle with icing (confectioners') sugar and place under a very hot grill/broiler to brown — keep an eye on it, as it can burn very suddenly!

Lemon Tart

In Listowel Co. Kerry, Armel Whyte and Helen Mullane run their delightful bar and bistro, Allo's. Armel's cooking and Helen's charming service make a winning combination. This tart is surprisingly different from the previous recipe as it contains a high proportion of lemon, including the grated zest, which makes it really tangy. Makes one 8-9"/20-23 cm flan.

Pastry
9 oz/250g/2¼ cups plain (all-purpose) flour
3 oz/75g/¾ cup icing (confectioners') sugar
4½ oz//125g/1¼ sticks butter, diced
grated zest of ½ lemon
grains from ½ vanilla pod
1 small egg

Put all pastry ingredients into a food processor and process at maximum speed until the mixture forms a ball. Wrap in clingfilm and chill for 1 hour. Then remove from the fridge and leave for 20 minutes.

Lemon Filling
5 small eggs
7 oz/200g/1 cup caster (superfine) sugar
zest of 1 lemon
juice of 2½ lemons
5 fl oz/150 ml/generous 1 cup double cream, whipped

Whisk the eggs with the sugar and zest, then stir in the lemon juice. Fold in the whipped cream. Remove any froth from the top.

To assemble
Line an 8-9"/20-23 cm flan case or loose-based tart tin with the pastry. Prick it lightly with a fork. Lay a sheet of grease-proof/waxed paper or foil and some baking beans on it and bake the pastry case blind, without browning, in a moderate oven preheated to 300°F/150°C/gas 2.
   Pour in the cold lemon filling and return to a cool oven, set at 250°F/130°C/gas ½ . Bake for 30 minutes, until the filling has set. When cooked, dust with icing (confectioners') sugar and serve warm or cold, with cream.

Blackberry & Apple Pie

Newport House in Co. Mayo is famous first and foremost for its fishing, although the warmth of its hospitality would come a close second — and with it, chef John Gavin's cooking. They are proud of their organic garden where a lot of the produce used in high season is grown. Although the dining style is fairly formal, John isn't afraid of simplicity, as you can see from this luscious early autumn pie. Serves 6-8.

Sweet Flan Pastry

5 oz/150g/1¼ sticks unsalted butter, at room temperature, cubed
3 oz/75g/3 US tbsp caster (superfine) sugar
1 tsp/1¼ US tsp vanilla sugar
pinch of salt
2 oz/50g/⅓ cup ground almonds (optional)
9 oz/250g/2¼ cups plain (all-purpose) flour
1 egg
½ tsp cold water

Put the butter, sugars, salt, almonds (if used) and flour all together in a food processor and run the machine for 15 seconds. Add the egg and water and blend until the pastry comes away from the side of the bowl. Wrap in clingfilm and leave in the fridge to rest, preferably overnight.

Filling

2 lb/900g cooking apples
6 oz/175g/6 US tbsp sugar
pinch each of cinnamon and cloves
8 oz/225g blackberries

milk or egg and milk, to glaze
granulated sugar, to dust

Peel and chop the apples. Put into a pan and cook gently with the sugar and spices (the apples will make their own juice), adding the blackberries when the apple is tender. Remove from the heat and leave to cool.

To assemble and cook

Preheat a fairly hot oven, 400°F/200°C/gas 6.

Cut off a good ⅓ of the pastry and reserve for the top. Roll the rest out fairly thinly and use it to line an 8-9"/20-23 cm pie plate or tart tin.

Arrange the filling in the middle of the pastry and dampen the edges with a little water. Roll out the reserved the pastry and lay it on top of the filling. Seal the edges between finger and thumb, or using a teaspoon handle and thumb. Make a little hole in the top to allow the steam to escape. Brush with a little milk or beaten egg and milk and sprinkle with granulated sugar. Put into the preheated oven and immediately reduce the temperature slightly to 375°F/190°C/gas 5. Bake for 30-40 minutes, until the pastry is crisp and golden-brown. Reduce the oven temperature during baking if the pastry shows signs of over-browning.

Serve hot, warm or cold in wedges, with whipped cream, home-made ice cream or crème fraîche and a sprig of mint to decorate.

Rhubarb & Gooseberry Pie

Right down on the waterside a few miles outside Athlone, Ray Byrne and Jane English's beautifully located Wineport Restaurant at Glasson is a charming and most unusual place with a sailing school, a semi-resident swan — and excellent food. Using local produce in its natural season is important to chef Noel Ryan. Since rhubarb and gooseberries are available at the same time, this is likely to be on the menu if you're there in early summer. They are two of the most easily-grown native foods in Ireland and very popular for home cooking. Serves 6-8.

Sugar Pastry
8 oz/225g/2 cups plain (all-purpose) flour
pinch of salt
5 oz/150g/1¼ sticks butter
2 oz/50g/2 US tbsp caster (superfine) sugar
1 egg, beaten

Filling
1½ lb/700g fruit (1 lb/450g rhubarb and ½ lb/225g gooseberries)
6 oz/175g/6 US tbsp caster (superfine) sugar
1 tsp ground ginger

milk, to glaze
caster (superfine) sugar, to dust

First, make the pastry. Sift the flour and salt into a mixing bowl. Cut in the butter and rub in until it reaches a sandy texture. Make a well in the centre.

Mix the sugar and beaten egg until the sugar has dissolved, then gradually incorporate it into the flour and butter mixture. Mix lightly to make a smooth paste. Bring together into a ball, wrap in clingfilm and chill for 1 hour before use.

Preheat a fairly hot oven, 400°F/200°C/gas 6.

Prepare the fruit. Trim and chop the rhubarb. Top, tail and halve the gooseberries. Mix the fruits together.

Roll out ½ the pastry and use it to line a greased 9½"/24 cm tart tin. Press in gently but firmly all round. Spoon in the mixed fruit and sprinkle evenly with the caster (superfine) sugar and ginger.

Roll out the remaining pastry to form a lid. Dampen the edges of the bottom layer of pastry, then arrange the top layer in position and press firmly all round to seal the edge. Trim the edges with a knife. Use the trimmings to make decorative leaves or flowers, if you like. Make a cross in the middle of the lid to allow steam to escape. Brush the top of the pie with milk and sprinkle with caster (superfine) sugar.

Bake for 30-40 minutes, until the pastry is crisp and golden-brown and the fruit is tender. Serve hot in wedges with home-made ice cream or whipped cream.

*Leftover pastry from any of these recipes can be used to make little tartlets filled, for example, with fresh cream and fruit or lemon curd.

Blackberry & Apple Crumble

Lindy and Brian O'Hara's Co. Sligo country house, Coopershill, is verging on the downright luxurious, but Lindy is a very down-to-earth person and, to the delight of guests, produces real country cooking for them, like this deliciously simple crumble. Serves 4.

Fruit mixture
8 oz/225g blackberries
1 lb/450g cooking apples
4 oz/100g/4 US tbsp sugar

Topping
4 oz/100g/1 cup plain (all-purpose) flour
2 oz/50g/2-3 US tbsp jumbo porridge oats
3 oz/75g/¾ stick butter
4 oz/100g/½ cup brown sugar

First, prepare the fruit. Sort through and rinse the blackberries. Peel and slice the apples. Put into a 2-3 pint/1.2-1.8 litre greased baking dish, with the sugar. Mix well.

Preheat a moderate oven, 350°F/180°C/gas 4.

To make the topping, mix all the ingredients to make a rough dough-like mixture. Spread over the fruit, pressing down slightly. Bake for about 45 minutes, until the topping is turning brown. Serve hot with cream or ice cream.

Variations
Rhubarb, apricots or any fruit of your choice may be used instead.

Apple & Oatmeal Layer Cake

This is juicy, full of flavour and has plenty of texture. It's a particularly versatile recipe, as it can be eaten cold as a cake or — even better — as a hot pudding. Makes a 7"/18 cm cake, to serve 6.

Fruit purée
1-1½ lb/450-700g cooking apples
3-4 oz/75-100g/3-4 US tbsp sugar
½ tsp ground cinnamon
2 oz/50g/⅓ cups seedless raisins

Oatmeal cake
4 oz/100g/1 stick butter or polyunsaturated margarine
1 tbsp/1¼ US tbsp honey
12 oz/350g/2 cups flaked oatmeal
1 oz/25g/1 US tbsp demerara (granulated brown) sugar
grated rind and juice of 1 lemon
1 egg, lightly beaten

Peel, core and slice the apples. Cook with a few tablespoons of water until soft. Sweeten to taste. Beat in the cinnamon and raisins to make a purée. Leave to cool.

Butter a 7"/18 cm cake tin, preferably loose-based. Preheat a fairly hot oven, 375°F/190°C/gas 5.

In a saucepan, melt the butter or margarine with the honey. Stir in the flaked oatmeal, demerara (granulated brown) sugar and the grated lemon rind. Lightly whisk the egg, mix with the lemon juice and blend thoroughly into the oat mixture.

Press ⅓ of the oat mixture into the base of the buttered tin. Cover with half of the apple mixture and repeat the layers, finishing with a layer of oats. Bake for about ½ hour, until cooked through and golden-brown.

Serve very hot with chilled crème fraîche, natural yogurt or vanilla ice cream, or serve cold with whipped cream as a cake.

Gaby's Cheesecake

At their cosy cottage near Cliffoney in Co. Sligo, Hans and Gaby Walter-Weiland lead an admirably self-sufficient life — baking bread from home-ground flour, making cheese, and this unusual speciality, a delicious baked continental cheesecake. The flavour improves if baked the day before use. Makes a 10"/26 cm cheesecake.

Base
5 oz/150g/1¼ cups wholemeal (whole-wheat) flour
2½ oz/60g/3 US tbsp honey or brown sugar
1 egg
2½ oz/60g/⅓ stick butter
1 spoonful water, if necessary

Filling
2¼ lb/1 kg quark (low-fat soft fresh cheese)
2-4 eggs (depending on size)
1 tsp/1¼ US tsp baking powder
4½ -5 oz/120-150g/5-6 US tbsp honey or brown sugar
handful of raisins
egg wash, to brush over

Preheat a moderate oven, 350°F/180°C/gas 4.

Prepare the base. Put all the ingredients into a food processor and chop and mix together to make a smooth dough.

Grease a 10"/26 cm spring-form tin and spread the dough over the base, making a raised edge of 1¼"/3 cm around the tin.

Mix all the filling ingredients together thoroughly. Turn onto the dough base in the tin and level it out. Brush with a little egg wash (egg yolk diluted with water) and bake for 1-1½ hours. Test for doneness with a dry skewer, which should come out clean and dry when the cheesecake is ready.

Carefully loosen the sides of the base from the tin with a knife. Open the spring clip on the tin and leave the cake in the tin for another 15-20 minutes to set. Transfer to a wire rack to finish cooling. Leave until the next day if possible, then serve in wedges — with whipped cream, if you like.

Festive Fare

The relentless rhythm of the changing seasons may not be quite as domineering in the kitchen these days, but it still has great influence. Most enthusiastic cooks enjoy baking in celebration of special dates and traditional festivals.

Christmas is the big one, of course, but Hallowe'en, Shrove Tuesday and Easter also have their own specialities and, as the holidays seem to grow, there's more time and motivation to bake something special for family and friends. These are also the times when we tend to do most entertaining, so some of the 'dressier' cakes and gâteaux are included at the end of this section.

Christmas

Traditional baking provides the culinary milestones that mark our progress towards Christmas — and the comforting feeling that at least some of the preparation is under control, well ahead of the rush.

As it needs longest to mature and allow the flavours to mellow, Christmas pudding starts the cycle. Prudent housewives used to make sure their puddings were made before September was out, but nowadays most people don't get around to thinking about it until Hallowe'en time. As puddings keep so well in a cool, dark place (no need to freeze), making enough for a two-year cycle is a good idea.

After the puddings, rich fruit cakes take the stage, needing a month or so to mature. Then come mincemeat and mince pies, which are most convenient frozen uncooked and baked straight from the freezer.

Traditional Christmas Pudding

This is one of the best hot desserts in the world and a treat at any time during the colder part of the year. Although steaming is the usual cooking method, it has its disadvantages — not only a steamed-up kitchen, but also the possibility of the pan either going off the boil or boiling dry. Baking — or, more correctly, 'oven-steaming' — is a better, more reliable method and, like the suggestion for using an electric slow-cooker given here, it can be applied to any normal recipe. This pudding is richly flavoured and packed with fruit, but it is also light, as it contains only breadcrumbs and no flour. Makes two 2-pint/1 litre puddings, each serving 6-8.

12 oz/350g/2 cups raisins
8 oz/225g/1½ cups currants
8 oz/225g/1⅓ cups sultanas (dried green grapes)
4 oz/100g/¾ cup glacé cherries
4 oz/100g/⅔ cup chopped candied peel
3 oz/75g/⅔ cup blanched, slivered almonds
14 oz/400g/3¾ cups fresh white breadcrumbs
1 small coffee-spoon/⅛ US tsp salt
1 tsp/1¼ US tsp ground mixed spice
1 tsp/1¼ US tsp ground cinnamon
1 tsp/1¼ US tsp finely grated nutmeg
½ tsp ground ginger
½ tsp ground cloves
8 oz/225g/1 cup shredded suet
8 oz/225g/1 cup demerara (granulated brown) sugar
1 good carrot, about 6 oz/185g, scraped and coarsely grated
1 large Bramley apple, 6-8 oz/175-225g, peeled and finely chopped or
    coarsely grated
finely grated zest and juice of 1 orange (washed)
finely grated zest and juice of 1 lemon (washed)
2 tbsp/2½ US tbsp black treacle (molasses)
4 fl oz/100 ml/½ cup whiskey, rum or brandy
4 eggs, lightly whisked

Sort through the dried fruit to remove any stalks or pieces of grit. Wash, dry, and halve the cherries. If using whole candied peel, cut up finely with a very sharp knife. Blanch and sliver the almonds. Remove crusts from a day-old white loaf of bread and make crumbs in a food processor or blender. Peel and grate the carrot and apple.

In a large bowl, mix all dry ingredients, including apple, carrot and grated lemon and orange zest.

Warm the treacle/molasses slightly in the microwave or small pan to make it runny and add the orange and lemon juice, liquor and the lightly beaten eggs. Mix the liquids well, add to the pudding mixture and stir to mix thoroughly.

Cover the bowl with a tea/dish towel and leave in a cool place overnight.

Next day, butter two 2-pint/l-litre pudding basins/round-sided bowls and put a buttered disc of greaseproof paper in the base of each. Prepare buttered double circles of greaseproof/waxed paper which are just a little larger than the tops of the bowls. Prepare double circles of plain greaseproof/waxed paper which are about 4"/10 cm bigger than the tops of the bowls.

Give the pudding mixture a good stir. Spoon into the prepared bowls and tap sharply on the worktop to eliminate air pockets. Smooth down the top with the back of a tablespoon, cover with the smaller buttered circles of greaseproof/waxed paper and tuck in neatly around the edge. Then lay the larger pieces of plain paper on top and tie down firmly with good string — allow enough for a handle, as it will be much easier and safer to handle the hot puddings later on. Trim the excess paper a bit if it is too bulky, then top off with a piece of foil and tuck it firmly under the rim of the bowl.

Cook by one of the following methods, then reheat when required by steaming/boiling for a further 2-3 hours.

Variations

The mixture given can be used to make one large, one medium and one small pudding, if more convenient; adjust cooking times according to size.

* To bake/oven-steam

This method is most reliable. The temperature is steady and the water does not require regular topping up, making it suitable for overnight cooking. It also keeps the kitchen free of steam. Preheat a very moderate oven, 300°F/150°C/gas 2. Stand the puddings in a deep roasting tin, ¾ full with boiling water. Cover everything completely with foil, joining the edges tightly to prevent steam escaping. Cook for about 6 hours, or overnight, reducing the temperature to 280°F/140°C/gas 1 if it will be left unattended for more than 6 hours.

* Electric slow cooker

If using this method, cook one pudding at a time. Select a bowl which comfortably fits your slow cooker without raising the lid. Unless otherwise recommended by the manufacturer, stand the pudding in the preheated cooker, add enough boiling water to come ⅔ up the side of the basin, cover and cook on HIGH for 13 hours. To reheat, allow about 5 hours.

* To boil: Stand puddings on trivets in deep saucepans. Pour in enough boiling water to come ⅔ of the way up the sides. Cover everything tightly and boil for 5-6 hours, making sure the water never goes off the boil and topping up regularly with boiling water to keep up a level at least half way up the bowl.

* Steam for 5-6 hours over pans of simmering water, making sure it does not go off the boil and topping up with boiling water as necessary.

* Pressure cooking is also suitable and much faster, although only one pudding can be cooked at a time. Consult your pressure cooker instruction leaflet for details, as these vary.

* Microwave cooking is also successful, especially in a ring mould. Adjust time to suit the power of your machine, based on the fact that half of the above mixture takes 16 minutes in a 700-watt microwave, on full power, plus an extra 2 minutes at the end when turned out upside-down on a plate. In my experience, microwaved puddings do not have the same keeping qualities as traditionally cooked ones, so I suggest either making them nearer the time of use or freezing them until required, then defrost and reheat on full power, allowing 1 minute per 1 lb/450g. The microwave is especially useful for reheating, as leftovers can be moulded — into individual ramekins, for example, or a ring mould — for attractive presentation the second time around.

Christmas Cake

If you like a traditional rich fruit cake, make up the medium-sized cake (9"/23 cm round/8"/20 cm square) given in the Wedding Cake recipe (page 111). Make at least a month before Christmas. (Traditional Almond Paste and Royal Icing are on pages 127.)

Quick Christmas Cake with Glazed Fruit & Nut Topping

For a simpler alternative, this is perfect — ideal when the baking has been left a little too late to allow rich cakes to mature. Although it keeps very well and cuts better if allowed to sit for a week or so before use, this attractive cake, which is well suited to people who dislike royal icing, can be used almost immediately.

Cake
½ pint/300 ml/1¼ cups cider
6 oz/175g/1½ sticks butter, at room temperature
7 oz/200g/1 cup soft dark brown sugar
8 oz/225g/2 cups plain (all-purpose) flour, sifted
pinch of salt
1 rounded tsp each mixed spices (cinnamon, cloves, ginger, nutmeg)
½ level tsp baking powder
4 oz/100g/¾ cup glacé cherries
4 oz/100g/2/3⅔ cup chopped mixed peel
1 ¼ lb/550g/3 cups mixed dried fruit (8 oz/225g/1 ½ cups currants,
    6 oz/175g/¾ cup each raisins and sultanas)
grated zest of 1 washed orange and/or 1 washed lemon
1 tbsp/1 ¼ US tbsp black treacle (molasses)
3 large eggs
2-3 oz/50-75g/½ -⅔ cup flaked almonds
2-3 oz/50-75g/½ -⅔ cup ground almonds
½ tsp vanilla essence
a few drops real almond essence

Topping
3-4 oz/75-100g/½ -¾ cup cherries or other glacé fruit
3-4 oz/75-100g/½ -¾ cup whole nuts, eg walnuts and Brazil nuts

Glaze
½ pint/300 ml/1¼ cups cider
4 oz/100g/4 US tbsp caster (superfine) sugar

Butter and base-line a 7"/18 cm square or 8"/20 cm round loose-based cake tin. Preheat a slow oven, 300°F/150°C/gas 2.

Prepare the cake.

Put the cider into a small pan and bring to the boil. Then reduce the heat and leave to simmer, uncovered, until reduced to about 4 tablespoons. Leave to cool.

Put all the other cake ingredients into a large mixing bowl. Mix well with a wooden spoon until thoroughly mixed, finally adding the reduced cider, a little at a time, until the right consistency is reached — the mixture should be quite stiff.

Turn the mixture into the prepared tin and smooth the top with the back of a tablespoon. Then arrange the topping nuts and glacé fruit lightly in rows on top of the cake — do not press into the cake mixture or they will sink during cooking.

Bake in the centre of the oven for 1 hour. Then reduce the temperature to 280°F/140°C/gas 1 and continue baking — protecting the top with a double sheet of greaseproof/waxed or brown paper if it becomes too brown at any stage — for another 1 ¼ hours, until the cake feels firm to the touch and is shrinking slightly from the tin.

To make the glaze

Put the cider and caster (superfine) sugar into a small pan and bring slowly to the boil, stirring. Reduce the heat and simmer fairly briskly, uncovered, until about 4 tablespoons of syrup are left. Brush this glaze over the hot cake and leave in the tin to cool. When absolutely cold, turn out and remove the base paper. Wrap lightly in fresh greaseproof/waxed paper and store in an airtight tin until required. To serve, set the cake on a board and decorate with ribbons.

Variations

*Glacé fruit will lose some of its bright colouring during baking. To retain the rich colouring, cook the cake without decoration and add the fruit and nuts when cold. The glaze given, or melted apple jelly, or warmed, sieved apricot jam, will hold them in place.

*A layer of almond paste can be laid under the fruit and nut decoration if you like (before or after baking). Or you can omit the fruit and nuts entirely and cover the cake with almond paste instead. Either decorate with the usual white icing or with almond paste cut-outs — Christmas trees, holly leaves, stars and moons — then toast it in the oven or under the grill/broiler instead of icing it.

Yule Log

For children, the most popular of all the seasonal cakes is the Yule log. Evocative of the great logs which were once brought into the hearth to burn throughout the festive period, this small cake is one of the most attractive Christmas foods. Children love it filled with whipped cream or butter icing, then covered with chocolate 'bark' icing. Add a sprig of holly, dust with icing (confectioners') sugar 'snow' and perch the traditional robin on top. First make the basic chocolate Swiss roll.

Chocolate Swiss Roll

2 oz/50g/4 US tbsp self-raising flour
1 oz/25g/2 US tbsp cocoa powder
3 eggs
3½ oz/90g/3½ US tbsp caster (superfine) sugar
extra caster (superfine) sugar, for rolling

Grease and base-line a Swiss roll/jelly roll tin about 13"x 9"/31 cm x 23 cm, allowing enough paper to extend beyond each end by about 1"/2.5 cm. Preheat a hot oven, 425°F/220°C/ gas 7.

Sift flour and cocoa powder together several times and set aside in a warm place on a sheet of greaseproof/waxed paper. In a bowl set over a pan of hot water, whisk eggs and sugar with an electric mixer or using a hand whisk until the mixture is very thick and foamy. If whisking by hand, this may take about 10 minutes. Then remove the bowl from the heat. Set it on a damp cloth to hold it steady and whisk for another 2 or 3 minutes.

Sift the cocoa-flour over the egg mixture, about a third at a time. Gradually fold it in gently with a metal spoon, trying to lose as little volume as possible.

Pour the mixture into the prepared tin, spread level and bake in the centre of the oven for 12-15 minutes, until well-risen and springy to the touch.

Lay a damp tea/dish towel on a work surface. Cover it with a sheet of greaseproof/waxed paper sprinkled evenly with caster (superfine) sugar. Turn cake onto the sugared paper. Peel the lining paper off the cake and, using a sharp knife, trim off the crisp edges to make it easier to roll. Roll up immediately, using the cloth as a guide. Leave the greaseproof paper inside; this prevents the cake from sticking together and makes it easier to unroll for filling when cold.

Meanwhile, prepare the Vanilla Butter Icing and Chocolate Butter Icing (page 128).

To assemble the Yule Log

Carefully unroll the cold Swiss roll and spread whipped cream or vanilla butter icing over the cake. Re-roll carefully, then use a palette knife to spread the chocolate butter icing on the outside of the Swiss roll. Use a fork or palette knife to mark circles on the ends. Along the top and sides, draw lines and knots to make the icing look like bark. Sprinkle lightly with icing (confectioners') sugar 'snow' and decorate with holly and, if you like, perch a robin on top.

Mincemeat with Irish Whiskey

This nice spicy mincemeat is not too sweet and has a good tang. A traditional recipe, it can be varied to make more unusual mixtures as long as the proportions are observed. Try substituting chopped dried apricots, peaches and prunes for the usual dried fruits, and experiment with different nuts and spicing. Although it will sometimes keep perfectly well for a year, mincemeat is really a short-term preserve. If you want to keep it longer than two or three months, try one of the variations at the end. Makes about 8 lb/3.6 kg.

3 lb/1.4 kg mixed dried fruit (sultanas, raisins, currants)
8 oz/225g/1½ cups cut mixed peel
4 oz/100g/¾ cup glacé cherries, chopped (optional)
1 lb/450g/2¼ cups dark muscovado (Barbados) sugar
1 lb/450g cooking apples (eg Bramleys), peeled and finely chopped
8 oz/225g/1 cup finely chopped suet
4 oz/100g/¾ cup almonds, blanched and slivered
1 ½ tsp/1¾ US tsp grated nutmeg
1 tsp/1¼ US tsp ground allspice
½ tsp each ground cinnamon and cloves
finely grated rind and juice of 2 juicy lemons (washed)
8 fl oz/225 ml/1 cup Irish whiskey

Mix all ingredients together in a large mixing bowl. Cover with a tea/dish towel and leave in a cool place for 24 hours, stirring occasionally. Mix well again before packing into clean, dry jars — preferably screw-top so that jars can be inverted occasionally to distribute the juices evenly. Seal and store in a cool, dark place for 2-4 weeks before use, inverting the jars from time to time if they are securely sealed. Any mincemeat left after Christmas will keep better if a little extra whiskey is added to the top of each jar.

Variations

*Baked Mincemeat
Mix all ingredients except the alcohol in an ovenproof bowl. Cover with a tea/dish towel and leave to stand overnight. Next day, remove the towel and cover with foil. Then cook in a very low oven, 225°F/110°C/gas ¼ for 3 hours. Cool, then mix in the whiskey and pot up. It will keep indefinitely if stored in a cool, dark place, although it may need some extra whiskey stirred in if it gets too dry.

*For a simpler alternative that looks more like ordinary fresh mincemeat, just cook the apple (it is usually raw apple juice that ferments and spoils the mincemeat) or use drier dessert apples such as Cox's instead.

Mincemeat Tarts with Streusel Topping

Some people find the proportion of pastry-to-mincemeat too high in traditional mince pies, but these are lighter and very attractive. Use quick Magimix Pastry (page 126) or One-Stage (Fork) Pastry (page 126). Both make a smooth, sweetened pastry which is easy to handle and cooks to a light, crisp golden-brown. Makes about 2 dozen.

> **1 quantity short pastry (as above)**
> **about 1 lb/450g mincemeat**

Streusel Topping
> **1 oz/25g/2 US tbsp plain (all-purpose) flour**
> **2 oz/50g/¼ cup light muscovado (Barbados) sugar**
> **1 oz/50g/¼ stick butter**
> **icing (confectioners') sugar, to decorate**

First, make up a batch of pastry. Chill for 30 minutes before use. While it is resting, prepare the streusel topping by rubbing the butter into the flour and sugar to form a crumb-like texture. Set aside.

Preheat a hot oven, 425°F/220°C/gas 7.

Roll out the pastry to about ⅛"/0.3 cm thick. Stamp out 24 bases, using a 3 ½ "/8.9 cm round fluted cutter. Use these to line the bases of 24 bun tins, then place about a teaspoonful of mincemeat in each one — be careful not to overfill, especially if the mincemeat is very juicy.

Sprinkle with the streusel mixture and bake immediately for about 20 minutes, until the pastry is a light golden-brown and the streusel is nice and crunchy. Using a round-bladed knife, ease the tarts from the tins and onto a rack. Dust with icing (confectioners') sugar and serve warm with chilled whipped cream, rum butter or brandy butter.

Variations

*Traditional Mince Pies

Made as above, except with pastry lids, these can be made up at any time and kept in the freezer, uncooked, to serve hot from the oven at very short notice.

As the pastry will probably need re-rolling to make all the bases and lids, cut out the lids first using a smaller cutter (2½ "/6.3" diameter). Re-roll as necessary, then cut out the bases and fill as above. Using a pastry brush dipped in cold water, dampen the edges of the lids and press them down gently onto the pastry bases. (An upturned egg cup can be useful for this.) Either bake as above or open-freeze, then wrap and store in the freezer until required.

To bake from frozen, put into a hot oven straight from the freezer, as for fresh mince pies, but allow about 10 minutes extra cooking time.

*Bite-Sized Mince Pies

Another nice idea is to make these little morsels. I came across them up at that great source of good home-cooking, Mitchells of Laragh, where they make them up in little tartlet tins. They're just big enough to pop into the mouth in one go, like petits fours — delicious with a dollop of rum butter tucked under the lid.

Mincemeat Lattice Pie

If making individual pies seems too fiddly, try this pie, either for Christmas or to use up any remaining mincemeat in the New Year. With its almond pastry base and citrus flavoured filling, it makes an excellent hot dessert. Serves 8-10.

Almond Pastry

10 oz/275g/2¼ cups plain (all-purpose) flour
2 oz/50g/⅓ cup ground almonds
6 oz/175g/1½ sticks butter
3 oz/75g/¾ cup icing (confectioners') sugar
finely grated zest of ½ lemon (washed)
yolk of 1 large egg, lightly beaten
1 coffee-spoon/¼ US tsp natural almond essence (or to taste)
3 tbsp/3¾ US tbsp very cold water
1 tbsp/1¼ US tbsp lemon juice

Filling

about 1 lb/450g home-made mincemeat
2 oz/50g/⅓ cup ground almonds
finely grated zest of ½ lemon (washed)
lemon juice (see method)
2 tbsp/2½ US tbsp Cointreau or Grand Marnier
1 egg white, beaten lightly, to glaze
caster (superfine) sugar, to sprinkle

First make the pastry. Put the flour, ground almonds and roughly chopped butter into the bowl of a food processor and process for a few seconds until the mixture looks like coarse breadcrumbs. Add the sugar and finely grated lemon zest. Mix together the egg yolk, almond essence, cold water and lemon juice. Add most of this to the bowl and continue to process until the mixture forms a ball around the centre of the chopping knife. Add the rest of the liquid, if necessary. Remove the pastry, wrap in clingfilm and leave in the fridge for at least 10 minutes before rolling.

Meanwhile, preheat a fairly hot oven, 400°F/200°C/gas 6.

Mix together the mincemeat, ground almonds, grated lemon zest, whatever lemon juice remains from the pastry and the Cointreau or Grand Marnier. Put this mixture aside.

Roll out the pastry to line a 9"-10"/22-25 cm fluted flan ring or a tart tin with removable base. Re-roll any remaining pastry and cut into long, thin strips. Spread the prepared filling over the base of the flan and arrange the strips of pastry in a lattice pattern on top. Brush the pastry with lightly whisked egg white and sprinkle with a little caster (superfine) sugar. Bake for about 30 minutes, until the pastry is crisp and brown.

Serve hot with chilled whipped cream (flavoured, perhaps, with a little orange flower water), rum butter or Cumberland butter.

Christmas Biscuits

Macaroons

These festive morsels can be made the usual medium size to serve with tea or as an accompaniment to cold sweets or ices, or smaller as petits fours. Intensify the flavouring by replacing the vanilla with almond essence and adding a dash of Amaretto liqueur. Makes about 2 dozen large, 4 dozen petits fours.

rice paper, for lining

4 oz/100g/⅔ cup ground almonds
6 oz/175g/6 US tbsp caster (superfine) sugar
2 egg whites
1 tbsp/1¼ US tbsp rice flour, cornflour (corn starch) or arrowroot
½ tsp vanilla essence

split almonds or glacé cherries, to decorate

Line 2 large or 2 medium baking trays with rice paper. Preheat a moderately hot oven, 375°F/190°C/gas 5.

Mix the almonds and sugar. Add the unbeaten egg whites and cream the mixture very thoroughly with a wooden spoon. Add the flour and vanilla and mix well.

Fill the mixture into a forcing bag fitted with a ½ "/1 cm plain nozzle and pipe into rounds about 2"/5 cm across. Alternatively, use a teaspoon to pile small mounds of the mixture onto the rice paper and spread apart neatly. Press a split almond or half a glacé cherry into the centre of each macaroon. Bake 15-20 minutes, until lightly browned, risen and slightly cracked. Cut the rice paper to fit around each macaroon and cool on a wire rack. When cold, store in an airtight tin.

Star Biscuits

These pretty seasonal biscuits can be made in varying sizes and decorated as suggested below. They make nice little petits fours or, if prettily packed, an attractive small gift.

4 oz/100g/1 stick butter
4 oz/100g/4 US tbsp caster (superfine) sugar
1 egg yolk
½ tsp vanilla essence
5 oz/150g/1¼ cups plain (all-purpose) flour
2 oz/50g/generous ⅓ cup ground almonds
½ tsp mixed spice

Preheat a moderate oven, 350°F/180°C/gas 4. Select a number of star-shaped biscuit cutters (or other shapes) in various sizes.

Cream the butter and sugar together until pale. Beat in the egg yolk and vanilla essence until light and fluffy. Mix the dry ingredients together and blend into the creamed mixture to make a stiff dough.

Turn onto a floured worktop and knead lightly into shape. Roll out to about ¼"/0.6 cm thickness and cut out shapes as you wish. Place the biscuits on greased baking trays and bake for 12-15 minutes, until the biscuits are a light golden-brown. Cool on wire racks.

When cold, decorate with coloured glacé cherries, nuts, silver balls or a light sprinkling of icing (confectioners') sugar 'snow'.

Shrove Tuesday

Until relatively recently, the Lenten fast was taken so seriously in Ireland that it meant abstaining not only from meat but also eggs and all milk products. The tradition of making pancakes on Shrove Tuesday (the day before Ash Wednesday) came about as a practical way of using up the surplus eggs, milk and butter which would otherwise go to waste.

Most Irish families still make pancakes on Shrove Tuesday and the tradition of tossing pancakes not only survives but actually thrives, providing voter-friendly photo opportunities for politicians and commercial opportunities for the catering trade.

Older traditions are more sociable. The dubious honour of tossing the first pancake went to the eldest unmarried daughter whose luck in having 'the pick of the boys' depended on tossing it neatly. If she 'tossed the cake crooked' (when somebody jogged her elbow, for example), she had no chance of marrying in the coming year. If successful, she cut the pancake into as many pieces as there were guests and handed them round.

Sometimes, the mother's wedding ring was slipped into the batter used for the first pancake; the person who got the lucky slice would not only be first married but especially fortunate in their choice of husband or wife.

Although the Pancake Tuesday tradition is still very much alive, most cooks now make the pancake well-known in other countries, whereas the old Irish tradition is for buttermilk pancakes (page 107), made with or without eggs, according to availability.

Buttermilk Pancakes

1 lb/450g/4 cups plain (all-purpose) flour
1 tsp/1¼ US tsp bread (baking) soda
1 tsp/1¼ US tsp salt
4 eggs (optional)
1 dsp/1½ US tbsp golden (Karo) syrup (optional)
buttermilk, to mix

Sift the flour, soda and salt into a large mixing bowl and make a well in the middle. If using the eggs, beat them in to the flour mixture with the syrup, if using, and enough buttermilk to make a thick batter.

Heat a griddle or heavy frying pan and grease lightly with a little dripping. Drop spoonsful of the mixture onto the hot pan. Cook on one side until bubbles rise, then flip over and brown the second side. Serve immediately, sprinkled with sugar, or hot-buttered with honey or home-made jam.

Easter

'Hot cross buns! / Hot cross buns!
One a penny, two a penny / Hot cross buns!'

Hot Cross Buns

Currarevagh House is in a lovely waterside location at Oughterard in Connemara. It's doubly famous for its fishing and June Hodgson's afternoon teas. These are her Hot Cross Buns, traditionally a Good Friday speciality but delicious at any time. Makes about 20 buns.

1 level tbsp/1¼ US tbsp dried yeast
¼ pint/150 ml/½ cup warm water
1 level tsp/1¼ US tsp caster (superfine) sugar
1 lb/450g/4 cups plain (all-purpose) flour
2 oz/50g/½ stick butter or margarine
¼ pint/140 ml/½ cup warm milk
1 egg, beaten
1 level tsp/1¼ US tsp salt
1 level tsp/1¼ US tsp mixed spice
2 oz/50g/2 US tbsp caster (superfine) sugar
1 oz/25g/⅓ cup raisins
2 oz/50g/½ cup mixed peel

Mix together the dried yeast, warm water and caster (superfine) sugar and leave for about 2 hours, until it has doubled in volume. Then sprinkle it onto 4 oz/115g/1 cup of the flour. Mix and leave for another 15 minutes to froth up.

Melt the margarine and add it to the yeast mixture, together with the warm milk and beaten egg. Mix the salt, mixed spice and caster (superfine) sugar with the rest of the flour and fold in to the yeast mixture, together with the raisins and mixed peel. Mix well.

Knead the dough on a floured surface and form into about 20 buns. Spread them out on greased and floured baking trays, making sure there is plenty of space between them. Leave to rise in a warm place.

Preheat a fairly hot oven, 375°F/190°C/gas 5.

When the buns have risen to twice their original size, slash each one on top in the shape of a cross and bake for 10-15 minutes.

During cooking, brush the buns with a glaze made of 1½ oz/ 40g/1½ US tbsp caster (superfine) sugar dissolved in 2 tbsp warm water. Remove from the oven when they are baked to a glossy golden-brown and cool on a wire rack. Use on the day of baking.

Simnel Cake

This was originally associated with Mothering Sunday, celebrated in Ireland in February. In recent times, however, it has become an Easter speciality and is often decorated as below, with eleven marzipan balls to represent the apostles, less Judas. This is a classic recipe for one of my favourite cakes — everyone loves the layer of gooey almond in the centre.

Marzipan
8 oz/225g/1 cup caster (superfine) sugar
8 oz/225g/1¾ cups icing (confectioners') sugar
l lb/450g/2⅔ cups ground almonds
2 eggs (or 4 yolks)
3 tsp/3¾ US tsp lemon juice
l tsp/1¼ US tsp almond essence

Cake
8 oz/225g/2 cups plain (all-purpose) flour
½ tsp salt
l salt-spoon/scant ⅛ US tsp each nutmeg, cinnamon and allspice
6 oz/175g/1½ sticks butter
6 oz/175g/1 cup soft dark brown sugar (Barbados)
3 eggs, lightly beaten
l lb/450g/3 cups currants
8-12 oz/225-350g/1½ -2 cups sultanas (dried green grapes)
4 oz/100g/2/3 cup chopped candied peel
scant ¼ pint/150 ml/½ cup milk
l level tbsp black treacle (molasses)

Topping
a little apple jelly or apricot jam
egg yolk beaten up with a little oil, to glaze

To make the marzipan
Mix sugars and almonds together in a large bowl. Make a hollow in the centre and drop in the lightly beaten eggs (or yolks), lemon juice and almond essence. Mix to a stiff paste, first with a wooden spoon, then with hands dusted with icing (confectioners') sugar. Knead well until smooth and free from cracks. (Or do all this very quickly in a Kenwood chef, using the K beater.) If possible, leave the ball in a polythene bag in the fridge overnight. Then leave to reach room temperature

again before use; it will then be easier to handle.

Preheat a slow oven, 300°F/150°C/gas 2. Butter and line a deep 8"/20 cm round cake tin, preferably loose-based.

To make the cake

Sift the flour, salt and spices together. Cream butter and sugar until light and fluffy. Add the lightly beaten eggs, a little at a time, including a spoonful of the sifted flour and beating well after each addition. When the mixture is thoroughly beaten, lightly stir in the remaining flour and then the fruit. Add just enough of the milk to make a fairly stiff batter (like a Christmas cake) and the treacle/molasses.

Divide the marzipan unevenly in half and roll the smaller piece to the exact size of the inside of the cake tin. Turn half of the cake mixture into the tin, level it out and cover with the circle of marzipan. Cover with the rest of the cake mixture, smooth down with the back of a spoon and bake in the centre of the oven for about 3 ½ hours, until the top is springy to the touch and the cake is shrinking slightly from the tin. A skewer should come out of the cake clean, but the marzipan in the middle makes this method less reliable than usual, so be careful not to put the skewer through it.

Cool the cake in the tin. When cold, turn out, remove papers and brush the top with a little warmed apple jelly or apricot jam, sieved if necessary, and place the second circle of marzipan on top, pressing down well.

Mark the top into squares ½ -1"/2-2.5 cm wide with a sharp knife and make eleven small balls from the marzipan trimmings. Arrange these around the edge of the cake and brush the marzipan lightly with beaten egg.

Put the cake into a hot oven or under the grill/broiler for a few minutes until toasted to a deep golden-brown. Alternatively, another traditional finish is to run a small pool of pastel coloured icing, preferably yellow, into the centre of the marzipan. In either case, it can also be decorated with a few tiny marzipan or foil-covered chocolate eggs and/or Easter chicks — children love these.

Easter Biscuits

As well as Simnel Cake and Hot Cross Buns for Good Friday, Easter would not be complete without my mother's big spiced biscuits. There is a tradition in some families of piping a cross of glacé icing on top, but ours were always left plain. Makes about 3 dozen.

1 lb/450g/4 cups plain (all-purpose) flour
1 level tsp/1¼ US tsp salt
1 level tsp/1¼ US tsp each ground cinnamon and mixed spice
8 oz/225g/2 sticks butter, at room temperature
8 oz/225g/1 cup caster (superfine) sugar
2 large eggs, beaten
6 oz/175g/1¼ cups currants
2 oz/50g/⅓ cup candied peel, chopped
milk, as required
1 egg white, lightly beaten, or a little extra milk, to glaze
granulated sugar, to sprinkle

Sift the flour, salt and spices together. Cream the butter and sugar until light and fluffy. Beat in the eggs and add, alternately, the currants and chopped peel and the dry ingredients. Mix to a stiff dough, adding a little milk if necessary.

Make a ball with the dough, wrap in clingfilm and chill for at least 1 hour.

Preheat a fairly hot oven, 400°F/200°C/gas 6.

Flour a work surface and roll out the dough quite thinly. Prick all over with a fork and stamp into rounds with a large fluted cutter, 3½ -4"/9-10 cm diameter. Lay them on greased baking trays (they should not spread much, but leave a little room between them). Bake for 15-20 minutes, until they are just beginning to brown. Remove from the oven, brush the biscuits quickly with the lightly beaten egg white or milk and sprinkle with granulated sugar. Return to the oven for a few minutes until pale golden and crisp. Allow to cool on the trays for 5 minutes, then transfer to a wire rack. When completely cold, store in an airtight tin.

Hallowe'en Barm Brack

The brack is probably the most Irish of all cakes and gets it name from the word *breac*, meaning 'speckled'. Simple 'tea' bracks and their variations, based on soaked fruit and a raising agent such as baking powder, are made all year, while Barm Brack, which is made with yeast, is now mainly a Hallowe'en speciality.

Symbolic objects intended to divine the future are often included in bracks, notably a small silver coin, a button, a thimble, a chip of wood and a rag — all hygienically wrapped in foil these days. The ring signified early marriage, usually within the year; the coin wealth; the button, bachelorhood; and the thimble, spinster-hood. Bleak futures were foretold by the wood, which predicted a stormy marriage, and the rag, which indicated poverty.

The most unusual and romantic symbol was a tiny wooden boat, which signified that the recipient would make a journey to the Skellig rocks and lead a life of single blessedness!

Today the ring is usually the only object included, although even the commercial bakers still maintain that tradition. One well-known firm actually carried it to unusual lengths a few years ago by including real 9-carat gold wedding rings in some of their bracks as a promotional ploy!

The traditional yeast brack would have been made with fresh yeast, but this version — made with dried yeast with only one rising, in the tins — is much quicker to prepare. Makes two 7"/18 cm round bracks or two loaves.

1 lb/450g/4 cups plain (all-purpose) flour
½ tsp ground cinnamon
¼ tsp ground nutmeg
½ tsp salt
2 sachets easy-mix dried yeast
3 oz/75g/½ cup soft dark brown sugar
4 oz/100g/1 stick butter
½ pint/280 ml/1¼ cups lukewarm milk
1 egg, lightly beaten
8 oz/225g/1¼ cups sultanas (dried green grapes)
4 oz/100g/¾ cup currants
2 oz/50g/⅓ cup mixed chopped peel
rings etc. (optional)

Glaze
1 tbsp sugar
2 tbsp boiling water

Butter two deep 7"/18 cm diameter cake tins.

Mix the dry ingredients, including the yeast, in a large bowl and make a well in the centre. Melt the butter and mix with the lukewarm milk and lightly beaten egg. Turn into the bowl with the dry ingredients. Mix thoroughly to make a thick, smooth dough, then work in the fruit and peel and mix in well

Divide the mixture between the two buttered tins, pressing the foil-wrapped ring or other charms into each one, if it's for Hallowe'en. Cover with a tea/dish towel and leave in a warm place for 30 minutes - 1 hour to rise.

Meanwhile, preheat a hot oven, 400°F/200°C/gas 6.

When the cake has doubled in size, bake for about 45 minutes, until shrinking slightly from the tins. When ready, the brack will sound hollow when tapped.

Remove from the oven and brush over with the glaze. Return to the oven for about 3 minutes until the tops are a rich, shiny brown. Turn onto a wire rack to cool. Serve sliced and buttered. The brack keeps well, but is delicious toasted and served hot with cinnamon butter.

Caragh Lodge Wedding Cake

Bride Cake, a much simpler forerunner of today's rich Irish wedding cakes, symbolised future prosperity and happiness. Now, although the style of cake is open to personal preference (and a growing number of couples are opting for lighter alternatives), cutting the cake is still an important part of any wedding ceremony.

This traditional family recipe is from Mary Gaunt of Co. Kerry whose mother, Moira Curtin, passed it on to her. Now, Mary not only makes it for family weddings, but often makes the middle-sized cake for guests' afternoon tea, or as a Christmas cake. Their cake is square but if you prefer a round one, use tins a size larger (7"/18 cm; 10"/25 cm; 13"/33 cm). Remember that rich fruit cakes need time to mature, so bake at least 4-6 weeks before the wedding. It is a good idea to make the small cake first if you are nervous. Experienced bakers could probably bake the two smaller ones together and the large one separately.

Ingredients according to tin size (square):

6"/15 cm	9"/23 cm	12"/30 cm
Butter		
6 oz/175g/1½ sticks	12 oz/350g/3 sticks	1½ lb/700g/6 sticks
Soft brown sugar		
6 oz/175g/⅔cup	12 oz/350g/1½ cups	1 ½ lb/700g/2½ cups
Eggs		
3	6	12
Plain (all-purpose) flour		
8 oz/225g/2 cups	1 lb/450g/4 cups	2 lb/900g/8 cups
Mixed spice		
¼ tsp/1.25 ml	½ tsp/2.5 ml	1 tsp/5 ml

Salt
Pinch	¼ tsp/	½ tsp

Sultanas
8 oz/225g/1¼ cups	1 lb/450g/2½ cups	2 lb/900g/5 cups

Currants
4 oz/100g/¾ cup	½ lb/225g/½ 1½ cups	1 lb/450g/3 cups

Raisins
6 oz/175g/1 cup	12 oz/350g/2 cups	1 ½ lb/700g/4 cups

Cut mixed peel
3 oz/75g/½ cup	6 oz/175g/1 cup	12 oz/350g/2 cups

Glacé cherries
3 oz/75g/⅔ cup	6 oz/175g/1½ cups	12 oz/350g/3 cups

Chopped prunes
2 oz/50g/¼ cup	4 oz/100g/½ cup	8 oz/225g/1 cup

Chopped dates
2 oz/55g/½ cup	4 oz/100g/1 cup	8 oz/225g/1¾ cups

Golden (Karo) syrup
1 tbsp/15 ml/1¼ US tbsp	2 tbsp/30 ml/2 ½ US tbsp	4 tbsp/60 ml/5 US tbsp

Chopped almonds
2 oz/50g/⅓ cup	4 oz/100g/⅔ cup	8 oz/225g/1 ½ cups

Brandy
as required	as required	as required

Preparation

Measure out the butter and sugar. Sift the flour with mixed spice and salt. Along with the eggs, leave in a warm atmosphere for 7-8 hours, or overnight.

Measure out all the fruits. Add just enough brandy or other alcohol to barely cover and leave to soak overnight.

Meanwhile, grease the tins and line base and sides with a double layer of buttered greaseproof/waxed paper, which should extend at least 2"/5 cm above the top of the tins. Tie a thick band of folded brown paper, or newspaper, around the outside of the tins to protect the cakes during the long cooking.

To mix

Cream butter and sugar very well. Add eggs, one at a time, and beat well between additions. Add a little flour with the eggs if the mixture is inclined to curdle.

Add the fruit mixture (which will have absorbed the brandy and plumped up), syrup and almonds. Mix well, then add the flour. The mixture should drop slowly from a wooden spoon. Turn into the prepared tin(s) and smooth the top with the back of a spoon. Bake in the centre of a very cool oven, preheated to 300°F/150°C/gas 2, reduced to 275°F/140°C/gas 1 after ½ hour.

Accurate cooking times are impossible to give, as ovens vary considerably. As a rough guide, allow about 3-3 ½ hours for the smallest cake, 4-4½ for the medium and as much as twice that for the largest cake. The important thing is to keep an eye on the cakes, checking at regular intervals: after 1 hour for the small cake, after 2-3 hours for the larger ones. Be prepared to protect from over-browning by laying paper or foil loosely over the top.

When cooked, the cakes shrink slightly from the sides of the tin and the top should feel firm when pressed lightly with the fingers. A clean, warmed skewer thrust into the centre of the cake should come out clean, with no uncooked mixture clinging to it. If uncertain whether the cake is cooked through (particularly in the case of the largest one), a test plug can be removed from the centre of the cake.

Unless you have a large fan oven, which has the benefit of more even heat so the two smaller cakes could probably be cooked together, it is normally better to bake the cakes separately. Fan ovens cook more quickly than conventional ones but are inclined to dry cakes out. Consult your manufacturer's manual for guidance on temperature and timing.

Whatever oven is used, keep a close eye on progress and use your common sense.

Cool the cooked cakes in the tins, then remove the papers and turn upside down onto a board. Make a lot of small holes all over the base with a skewer and pour in some extra brandy — about 2-3 fl oz/60 ml/¼ cup for the small cake; 9 fl oz/250 ml/1 ¼ cups for the large one; and 7 fl oz/200 ml/2/3 cup for the medium one. When the brandy has been thoroughly absorbed, wrap the cold cakes in a double layer of greaseproof/waxed paper, then a layer of foil. Seal and store in a cool place for at least a month, until you are ready to finish the cake about a fortnight before the wedding.

Hints

* For a 3-tier wedding cake, a 3"/7.5 cm difference between tiers looks well-balanced, as given above. For a 4-tier cake, 2"/5 cm difference is enough. Cake boards need to be 1½ "-2" /3.5-5 cm bigger than the cake.

* If you have a favourite Christmas cake recipe and want to make a simple 2-tier cake, it can be adapted quite easily. Use the quantities given for an 8"/20 cm square or 9"/23 cm round cake for the base and halve them to make a square 6"/15 cm or round 7"/18 cm one for the top layer.

Desserts For Entertaining

Chocolate Fudge Terrine

This is from the Park Hotel in Kenmare, Co. Kerry and reminds me that this is a remarkable kind of place, where things are not always as you expect. Famous for unswerving dedication to the highest standards yet also for a relaxed atmosphere, it's just the kind of place where a rich chocolate terrine might end up on an afternoon tea tray. Makes ??

> 9 oz/250g/9 squares dark chocolate
> 9 oz/250g/2¼ sticks unsalted butter
> 9 oz/250g/1¼ cups caster (superfine) sugar
> ½ tbsp flour
> 5 eggs

Preheat a fairly hot oven, 375°F/190°C/gas 5.

Melt the chocolate and butter in a bowl over hot (not boiling) water. Add the sugar and stir well until dissolved. Whisk the flour and eggs until pale and creamy and fold into the chocolate mixture.

Line a terrine (1¾ pint/1 litre) with aluminium foil, pour in the mixture and put into a *bain marie* (roasting tin ⅔ full of hot water). Bake for 1 ½ hours. Leave to cool in the terrine.

To serve, turn out and peel off the foil lining. Serve neatly sliced, with either a Crème Anglaise (light egg custard sauce) or a strawberry or raspberry coulis. Garnish the plate with a sprig of mint leaves or fresh fruit and a light dusting of icing (confectioners') sugar.

Profiteroles with Caramel Topping

Up at Fahan on the Inishowen peninsula overlooking Lough Swilly, Reg Ryan and Phil McAfee have been delighting visitors to Restaurant St John's with their warm hospitality and good food for the best part of two decades. Although seafood probably takes centre stage, their baking and desserts are always particularly pleasing. Phil's recipe for profiteroles makes 60-70.

Profiteroles
½ pint/300 ml/1 ¼ cups water
2 oz/50g/½ stick butter
5 oz/150g/1 ¼ cups self-raising flour
4 small eggs (size 4), beaten

Caramel topping
¼ pint/150 ml/½ cup water
6 oz/175g/6 US tbsp granulated sugar

Filling
1 ½ pints/900 ml/3 ¾ cups cream
6 tbsp/7-8 US tbsp Irish Cream liqueur
2 tbsp/2 ½ US tbsp icing (confectioners') sugar

To make the profiteroles
Preheat a fairly hot oven, 400°F/200°C/gas 6.

Place the water and butter in a saucepan and bring to the boil. Place the flour on a piece of greaseproof/waxed paper and shoot it into the boiling liquid. Beat quickly with a wooden spoon until the mixture forms a ball. Place the mixture into the bowl of an electric mixer and, using the K beater (or equivalent), beat well, gradually adding the beaten eggs, a little at a time.

Lightly oil some large baking trays. Using a teaspoon, place small balls of the mixture at intervals on the trays. Sprinkle with water and cook in the hot oven for about 25 minutes, until well-risen and firm. Cool on a wire rack.

To make the topping
Put the water and sugar into a heavy saucepan and heat to dissolve the sugar. Then boil until the syrup turns brown at the edges. Remove from the heat and leave for a minute, until the syrup is free of bubbles. Pour quickly and lightly over the profiteroles on the cooling racks. Make a hole in the side of each profiterole.

To fill

Whip all the filling ingredients together until stiff. Using a piping bag and nozzle, pipe the cream into the side of each profiterole. Use within 3 hours. Do not store in the fridge, as the topping will soften.

Snow Roll with Lemon Curd

Ballyvolane is Jeremy and Merrie Green's eighteenth-century house on the River Blackwater in Co. Cork. It has many claims to fame, including magnificent gardens and woodland, as well as Merrie's skills as a ghillie (fishing guide) — and her cooking. Try this luscious dessert for yourself. Always delicious, it is perfect for Christmas time. Although Merrie suggests two whole eggs and two yolks for the lemon curd, it may be more convenient to use four yolks if you are making it at the same time as the snow roll. For the same reason, it's a good idea to make the lemon curd when making meringues, since the egg white isn't wasted. Serves 8.

Lemon Curd
grated rind and juice of 3 lemons
3 oz/75g/¾ stick butter
12 oz/340g/1½ cups caster (superfine) sugar
2 whole eggs
2 egg yolks

Snow Roll
5 egg whites
8 oz/225g/1 cup caster (superfine) sugar
1 tsp/1¼ US tsp white wine vinegar
1 tsp/1¼ US tsp vanilla essence
1 tbsp/1¼ US tbsp cornflour (corn starch)

Filling & decoration
icing (confectioners') sugar
½ pint/300 ml/1¼ cups cream
grapes, or other fresh fruit

First make the lemon curd. Place the grated lemon rinds, juice, butter and sugar in a heavy-based saucepan over a gentle heat. Stir occasionally, completely dissolving the sugar. Beat the eggs and extra yolks until well mixed, then pour a little of the hot lemon mixture onto the eggs and mix well. Pour the egg mixture into the pan with the rest of the hot lemon mixture and cook gently over low heat, stirring continuously, until the mixture thickens. Do not boil. Remove from the heat and pour into clean, warm jars while still hot.

To make the Snow Roll

Oil a Swiss roll/jelly roll tin and line it with baking parchment. Preheat a moderate oven, 350°F/180°C/gas 4.

Whisk the egg whites until very stiff and continue beating while adding the caster (superfine) sugar, a spoonful at a time. Add the vinegar, vanilla essence and cornflour/corn starch and mix thoroughly. Spoon the mixture into the prepared tin and spread evenly, right to the edges. Bake for 15 minutes, then remove from the oven and allow to cool.

Dust a sheet of greaseproof/waxed paper with icing (confectioners') sugar and turn the snow roll onto it.

For the filling

Whip the cream until stiff, then fold in about 3 tbsp of the lemon curd. Spread it evenly onto the snow roll and, using the greaseproof paper to help you, gently roll it up. Transfer the roll to a serving plate.

To finish

Pipe whipped cream onto the top and sides and decorate with halved and pipped/pitted green and black grapes, or other fresh fruit.

Ballymaloe Walnut Meringue

The dessert trolley at Ballymaloe is always laden with temptations and often includes this meringue, a long-time favourite dessert that can be baked either as a meringue gâteau (given here) or to make individual meringue halves for pairing. Although the filling can be varied, fresh pear slices and whipped cream complement the walnuts especially well. Free-range eggs are always used at Ballymaloe and it's interesting to note that they produce greater volume than battery eggs when whisked. Leftover yolks could be used to make a large quantity of sauce, such as a deep yellow mayonnaise, or lemon curd (as above).

Meringues
4 egg whites
8 oz/225g/1 cup caster (superfine) sugar
10-12 walnut halves, chopped

Filling
½ pint/300 ml/1¼ cups cream
2 ripe pears, peeled and sliced

Preheat a very cool oven, 275°F/140°C/gas 1. Line 2 baking sheets with Bakewell paper (a little dot of white cooking fat under the corners will hold it down) and lightly mark out two circles about 8-9"/20-23 cm diameter.

Beat the eggs until stiff but still wet looking. Stir in half of the sugar, then beat until very stiff and dry. Fold in the remaining sugar and add the chopped walnuts.

Spread or pipe the mixture to make equal rounds on the Bakewell paper. Bake slowly in the cool oven. They should not rise at all — if they do, the oven is too hot. When ready, they will be lightly coloured and dried out and the parchment will peel away easily without sticking. Remove parchment and cool on wire racks. When cool, fill with whipped cream and fresh pear slices.

Variation

Fill and decorate in any way you like. For example, whip ½ pint/280 ml/1¼ cups cream until thick. Flavour with a little vanilla essence or an appropriate liqueur, such as Baileys. Use a good half of the cream to sandwich the layers together, spread the rest on top and dot with walnut halves.

Amaretti Dacquoise

Triple House Restaurant at Termonfeckin, Co. Louth, serves this marvellous meringue dessert which would be ideal for a dinner party. Pat Fox makes it with whatever soft fruit is in season.

For the dacquoise/meringue

5 size-1 egg whites (7 fl oz/200 ml/⅔ cup)
8 oz/225g/1 cup caster (superfine) sugar
3/4oz /20g/about ½ cup amaretti (almond) biscuits, ground
½ oz/10g/1 US tbsp walnuts, broken into small pieces by hand
½ soup-spoon/1 US tbsp Bournville (semi-sweet) cocoa, sifted

Filling

½ pint/300 ml/1¼ cups cream
1 1 /2 oz/35g/1½ US tbsp caster (superfine) sugar
1 dsp/1½ US tbsp dark rum

To decorate

1 ½ oz /35g/1 US tbsp praline (see below)
6 oz/175g fresh ripe redcurrants, de-stalked

Preheat oven to 400°F/200°C/gas 6. Line 2 baking trays with parchment, pencil in two 9"/23 cm circles and brush with clear melted butter.

To make the meringue, whip the egg whites until soft peaks form. Then, still beating, add all the sugar and continue beating until fully risen and glossy. Put ⅓ of this mixture into a large bowl with the amaretti, walnuts and sifted cocoa. Mix thoroughly with a metal spoon. Tip remaining meringue mixture in and carefully fold in with a wire whisk. Divide the mixture between the two 9" circles and spread evenly to the pencilled edges with a spatula.

Turn the oven down to 350°F/180°C/gas 4 and bake on two shelves for 30 minutes. Change shelves, then bake for a further 15 minutes. Remove and leave to cool.

* Temperature and times are based on a large old gas oven (non- convection), so adapt as necessary to suit other types.

To make the filling

Whip the cream to soft peaks, add sugar and rum and whip until stiff. Spread this on one 9" dacquoise and then sprinkle the praline and redcurrants on top. Cover with the second dacquoise and gently press down to fit. Refrigerate for 30 minutes to 1 hour to make slicing easier.

To make praline

Caramelise 6 oz/175g/6 US tbsp caster (superfine) sugar in a dry pan. Add 6 oz/175g/1 cup chopped nuts (*not* walnuts). Cook for 2 minutes, then cool on an oiled slab of marble. When cold, grind to a powder. Keeps well in a screw-top jar.

Strawberry Kirsch Cake

They serve this luscious confection at Barberstown Castle, Co. Kildare.

1 x 10"/25 cm loose-based cake tin

8 oz/225g sweet flan pastry (page 125)
1 x 7-egg sponge cake
2 oz/50g/2 US tbsp home-made strawberry jam
25 strawberries
flaked almonds, toasted and lightly crushed, to decorate
Kirsch Whipped Cream (see below)

On the morning before required for serving at dinner, bake the sponge cake and make the pastry.

Before assembly, prepare the whipped cream.

Kirsch Whipped Cream

3 egg yolks
15 oz/425g/1⅔ cups caster (superfine) sugar
1 pint/600 ml/2½ cups cream, whipped
3 leaves gelatine (or 1 sachet powdered gelatine)
4 ½ fl oz/120 ml/scant ½ cup dry white wine
1 fl oz/25 ml/1 US tbsp kirsch

Whisk the egg yolks and sugar until light and fluffy. Fold in the whipped cream. In a small pan, soften the gelatine in the white wine and add the kirsch. Then heat gently to dissolve. Put a little of the cream and egg yolk mixture into a small bowl or jug and quickly mix the gelatine mixture into it. Then, working fast, mix this into the rest of the whipped yolks and cream. Use as required to layer with the sponge cake and strawberries, as described.

To assemble

Preheat a fairly hot oven, 375°F/190°C/gas 5.

Roll the prepared pastry out thinly, to about ⅛"/3 mm thick, and use to line the base of the cake tin. Bake blind in the preheated oven for 10 minutes. Allow to cool, then spread the jam on top.

Cut the sponge into three layers and place one on top of the jam. Set a few of the strawberries aside for decoration. Slice the rest and arrange about ½ of them on the first layer of sponge. Spread about ¼ of the kirsch cream over the strawberries. Repeat with another layer of sponge, strawberries and kirsch cream. Then put the third layer of sponge on top and leave to set for 2 hours.

To serve, decorate the top and sides with the remaining whipped sweetened cream. Coat the sides with toasted almonds and decorate the top with the reserved strawberries.

Festive morsels – Star Biscuits (page 106) and Macaroons (page 105)

Opposite: Christmas Goodies – Mincemeat Lattice Pie (page 104) and Mincemeat Tarts with Streusel Topping (page 103)

Previous page: A luscious confection from Barberstown Castle – Strawberry Kirsch Cake (page 118)

For that special day – Caragh Lodge Wedding Cake (page 111)

Bring out the brandy to flambé this Traditional Christmas Pudding (page 98)

An irresistible temptation – Ballymaloe Walnut Meringue (page 116)

From the Park Hotel – A Rich Chocolate Fudge Terrine (page 113)

Full of tradition – The Hallowe'en Barm Brack (page 110)

Georgina Campbell's Quick Christmas Cake with Glazed Fruit & Nut Topping
(page 100)

A selection from the Shamrock range

Shamrock
The Most Natural Tastes in the World

Shamrock Foods has been associated with the unique and nostalgic pleasures of baking for many, many years. Who can forget childhood memories of helping to stir the sultanas or currants into the cake mixture? Or waiting eagerly for the bowl with the last bits of icing in it? Or even stealing a handful of raisins after they had been weighed for the pudding?

Shamrock Foods are no doubt best known for their wide range of dried and glacé fruits, nuts, sugars and flour. The Shamrock range also extends to such products as brown bread mixes, rices, pulses and tinned tomatoes.

The expert buyers from Shamrock Foods travel the world in their search for the finest quality products, offering you the choicest, finest ingredients for all your baking needs.

The Shamrock range of baking products includes the following:

Flours
Plain flour
Self-raising flour
Strong white flour
Howards 'Oneway' coarse
    wholemeal
Howards 'Oneway' extra coarse
    wholemeal
Howards brown bread mix
Abbey stoneground wholemeal
Mosses brown bread mix

Dried Fruits
Currants
Sultanas
Raisins
Fruit mix
Prunes
Figs
Apricots

Nuts
Almonds
Marzipan
Walnuts
Mixed nuts
Coconut

Cherries & Peel
Cherries
Mixed peel
Mixed glacé fruits

Sugars
Caster sugar
Golden Caster sugar
Golden Granulated sugar
Demerara sugar
Light muscovado sugar
Dark muscovado sugar
Ready-to-roll icing

Desserts
Custard
Semolina
Tapioca
Creamed rice pudding
Cornflour

Useful Information

Types of Sugar

Granulated sugar — the ordinary everyday sugar used in tea or coffee and with cereals. In the kitchen, for making syrups, sweetening poached fruits, in preserves and wine-making. Light, dry and free-flowing, with a smooth, granular texture. Ordinary refined white granulated sugar is most common, but it is also available in golden form.

Caster sugar — also light, dry and free-flowing but finer-grained than granulated sugar. Used mainly in cooking to cream smoothly with butter for making cakes and biscuits or to whisk with egg whites for meringues. Ideal for sweetening soft fruits and whipping cream for desserts. The most common form is refined white, but natural golden caster sugar is also available.

Demerara sugar — large, sparkling, golden-brown crystals and a crunchy, slightly sticky texture. Ideal for sweetening coffee or to sprinkle on foods when a crunchy texture is desirable, or for use in toppings for cakes and crumbles.

Light muscovado — the unrefined equivalent of light soft brown sugar. A pale brown fine-grained sugar with a slightly sticky texture. Can be used instead of caster sugar. Ideal where more flavour is required, as when making fudge.

Dark muscovado — the natural equivalent of refined dark soft brown sugar. Rich in natural molasses, which gives it a sticky texture, rich flavour and aroma. Ideal for baking, especially in rich fruit cakes and gingerbreads. Can also be used in savoury dishes, such as sweet and sour or barbecue sauces.

Flavoured sugars are useful to have ready. The simplest and most versatile is **vanilla sugar** — just leave a vanilla pod in a jar full of caster/superfine sugar. The sugar will absorb the flavour of the pod and be ready for use whenever vanilla flavouring is required.

Orange and lemon flavoured sugars: Grate the rind of an orange or lemon very finely and mix with 4 oz/100g/4 US tbsp caster/superfine sugar. Blend with a wooden spoon until the sugar is coloured. Then spread out on a sheet of greaseproof/waxed paper or foil and leave in a warm place until dried out. Crush any lumps and store in a screw-top jar.

Uses: In any recipe including sugar where a citrus flavour is appropriate (fruit compotes or pies). Flavouring plain sponge cakes, ice creams, custards and egg-based cold sweets such as Crème Caramel. In place of plain caster/superfine sugar on pancakes.

Dried Fruits

Dried fruits fall into two main categories, vine fruits and tree fruits. The most common fruits used in baking are vine fruits such as currants, sultanas and raisins, all of which are dried grapes. Currants, which have an intensely fruity flavour disproportionate to their tiny size, are produced from small seedless black grapes, while sultanas come from a seedless white (green) grape that originated in Turkey but which is now widely grown elsewhere. Raisins come from several types of grapes, mostly seedless white (green) grapes that are allowed to darken naturally for several weeks as they dry in the sun.

Glacé fruits, including peel (often referred to in recipes as mixed peel or chopped peel) come from tree fruits of the citrus family. The mixture varies but usually includes lemon and orange peel, sometimes also other citrus peel such as grapefruit and lime. Glacé cherries (usually coloured red to make them more appealing; also available in green, yellow and their natural colour, which is a muted red) are also tree fruits.

Other popular dried tree fruits commonly used in baking, for desserts and preserves, sauces and many other cooking purposes include prunes (dried plums), apricots, peaches, nectarines, apples, figs, dates, bananas and pineapple. All types of dried fruit are very nutritious, containing a concentration of natural fruit sugar (fructose), minerals and dietary fibre. Good quality dried fruits tend to be larger than others and look clean, blemish-free, fresh and plump. Pre-packed dried fruit is best bought in see-through packs enabling you to check the quality before buying and during storage — and re-sealable packs keep partly-used packs fresh for longer.

Types of Nuts

Almonds are available in shell but are more often shelled and sold in a variety of ways. Whole and split almonds are used in baking, either as they are or slivered. Flaked almonds are often toasted and used as a decoration, while chopped almonds are usually sprinkled over desserts and ice creams. Ground almonds add moistness and flavour to cakes and are also used for almond paste on rich fruit cakes and speciality biscuits such as macaroons. Whole almonds need to be blanched briefly in boiling water to loosen the skins, which then rub off easily. Although the bitter almond is used for essences and oils, the one used for cooking is the sweet almond.

Brazil nuts are large, creamy nuts with a high fat content. They are available in the shell, for cracking to eat raw with cheese and fruit, or shelled for use in sweet-making, salads, vegetarian dishes etc.

Cashew nuts are small, creamy-coloured kidney-shaped nuts, often sold salted to serve with drinks. Always sold shelled, they have a delicate, slightly sweet flavour and are an excellent addition to many dishes, including salads and Oriental foods such as curries and stir-fries.

Chestnuts come from the sweet chestnut tree (not the one common in Ireland) and are grown mainly in European countries, notably Spain. With a delicious rich flavour, chestnuts in their skins can be pierced and roasted, as in the traditional street food. Otherwise, they need to be skinned: slit the skin and soak in boiling water, then peel off both outer and inner skins before use in stuffings or soups or to serve whole with vegetables such as Brussels sprouts. Dried chestnuts are also available (soak for 30 minutes before use as fresh ones) and canned ones are available whole or as an unsweetened purée, or sweetened for use in desserts and gâteaux. The delicious sweetmeat, marrons glacés, is made from whole chestnuts preserved in syrup.

Coconut is available fresh (during the autumn), desiccated or creamed (sold in blocks) and is most often used in baking and Oriental cooking. Freshly grated coconut can be toasted in the oven as a decoration for cakes and puddings. Fresh coconut milk does not keep well (two days in the fridge) but desiccated coconut and the creamed blocks can be used to make a milk to use in curries.

Hazelnuts are native to the British Isles, although they are now seen less often. Cobs and filberts are from the same family. Available in the shell and shelled, they have a distinct flavour and are most often used in sweets, cakes and pastries; the flavour has a particular affinity with chocolate. Toasted hazelnuts are delicious in salads, particularly with a dressing that includes aromatic hazelnut oil.

Peanuts are rich in protein and highly nutritious. Available in many forms — plain shelled, roasted and salted, dry-roasted and ground in peanut butter. They are used mostly as snacks but can be added to salads or used in vegetable dishes. Peanut butter is used in satay sauces.

Pecans belong to the walnut family and can be used to replace walnuts in any recipe. They are flatter and smoother, with a slightly sweeter flavour than walnuts and are available in the shell and shelled.

Pine nuts (also known as pine kernels and pinoli) are the small, cream-coloured seeds of the Mediterranean pine tree. Always sold shelled, they are sometimes roasted and salted. Toasted to bring the flavour out, they make a delicious crunchy addition to salads and rice dishes; ground pine nuts are an essential ingredient of pesto, the Italian sauce made with basil.

Pistachio nuts have bright green kernels and are available salted, to eat as a snack, or plain, for use in the kitchen as a colourful and flavoursome ingredient in sweets, ice creams, pâtés and rice dishes. If plain ones are unavailable, salted pistachios can be used in some dishes if they are soaked to remove as much salt as possible before use.

Walnuts are grown in various parts of the world and are available both in the shell and shelled. Shelled walnuts are sold in halves (a distinctive, wrinkly dark brown), in broken pieces, chopped and sometimes ground. They have a moist, oily texture and slightly bitter flavour that works best in savoury dishes, although they are often used in sweet baking. Fresh, unripe green walnuts are sometimes available pickled in jars. The especially high oil content in walnuts can produce a rancid flavour in long storage, so they are best bought fresh.

Buying & storing nuts

Buy nuts frequently in small quantities and store in a cool, dark place, preferably in airtight containers in the fridge. Use as quickly as possible, certainly within 3 months. Nuts bought in the shell should feel heavy for their size — light ones are likely to be stale.

Toasting nuts, especially almonds, hazelnuts and pine kernels, enhances their flavour. Bake on a tray in a moderate oven for about 10 minutes, or under the grill or in a dry pan, turning frequently and watching closely to avoid burning.

Types of Flour

The most versatile flour for baking is wheat flour which absorbs liquid well. Elasticity in dough (its ability to stretch and rise to increase its volume and become lighter in texture) depends on the gluten content. This varies with the kind of wheat used and where it is grown.

Strong flour has a high gluten content and is very absorbent. Milled from hard wheat, mostly grown in North America. Ideal for making yeast breads, batters and pastries which need to rise (such as puff and choux) and also pasta.

Soft flour is grown in mild, damp climates such as Ireland. Has a lower gluten content. Suitable for some baking purposes, such as making biscuits, but is likely to be included in a blend.

Wholemeal (whole-wheat) flour is made from the whole of the wheat grain. To make white flour, the bran (husk) and wheat germ (embryo) are removed.

After milling, the various types of flours available include:

Plain flour, also known as household or all-purpose flour and, in Ireland, cream flour. Used most for general baking purposes. Milled from a medium blend. Suitable for baking cakes, scones and soda breads, short pastries etc. — everything except yeast baking.

Self-raising flour is a blend of plain/all-purpose flour and baking powder. Used mainly for cakes (especially quick all-in-one mixtures), buns and scones. Like soda bread mixtures, it has to be baked immediately after mixing or the baking powder, which reacts with liquids, loses its power.

Wholemeal flours are milled or stone-ground whole-wheat grains. Milled wheat can be coarse, medium or finely ground; stonemeal is usually coarsely ground. Usually blended with plain/all-purpose (white) flour for a lighter texture in breads and scones. Also known as whole-wheat, but not to be confused with wheatmeal.

Wheatmeal is a blend of white flour with bran and wheat germ, used for general baking purposes.

Gluten-free flour is used, with Soya flour added, to bake specialist products for coeliacs.

Granary flour is a wholemeal blend including malted wheat and rye.

Non-wheat flours — rye, cornmeal (Indian corn), oatmeal. Almost invariably mixed with wheat flour to make up for their lack of gluten. Traditional Irish oat recipes are an exception.

Bread mixes are proprietary mixtures of flours and raising agents that only need to be mixed with liquid.

Raising Agents

These work in various ways to lighten mixtures, open the texture and increase volume. The main raising agents are:

Bicarbonate of soda/bread soda/baking soda — Acid works with moisture in the dough to produce gas (carbon dioxide) which makes the dough rise. The acid is usually provided by:

buttermilk or sour milk (lactic acid). Sometimes yogurt is mixed with fresh milk with similar effect.

cream of tartar (Bextartar), used with fresh milk.

Baking powder is a mixture of bicarbonate of soda and an acid that works like cream of tartar to create gases which make the dough rise.

Mixtures including any of the above raising agents have to be baked immediately, before the gases escape.

Yeast is a living fungus. Once activated — by moisture, food (sugar) and warmth — it ferments, reproducing itself and creating gases that make the dough rise.

Fresh yeast is creamy in colour and texture. Keeps for a week in the fridge or up to three months in the freezer. Store, well-wrapped, in 1½ -2 oz/40-50g portions for batches of bread based on about 3 lb/1.4 kg flour.

Dried yeast can be kept in an airtight container at ordinary room temperature for up to six months. Only half the quantity is needed — ½ -1 oz/15-25g for a

3 lb/1.4 kg batch of bread. Needs extra sugar or honey (in addition to the natural sugars present in flour) to activate it. 'Easy-mix'/'fast-action' dried yeasts are sold in sachets (allow one sachet per 1 lb/450g flour) and add straight into the flour to make quick, short-cut bread recipes.

Recipes with a lot of fruit and nuts require extra yeast.

Temperature is crucial for yeast, which requires gentle warmth (around 80-82°F/27-28°C) during fermentation, then a very hot oven, which kills the yeast and prevents further growth.

Salt (1 tsp/1¼ US tsp per 1 lb/450g/4 cups flour) is also essential for yeast breads.

Leaf gelatine — Six sheets of leaf gelatine equal 1 oz/25g powdered gelatine. To use, wash in cold water, then soak in a bowl of cold water for 15-20 minutes until soft. Squeeze the softened gelatine lightly to remove surplus water, then put it into a bowl with the measured amount of liquid used in the recipe. Place the bowl over a pan of hot water and heat, without boiling, over a low heat until dissolved.

Powdered gelatine — usually sold in 2 oz/50g packets of 5 sachets, each containing 11g/0.4 oz or 3 level teaspoons — enough to set 1 pint/600 ml liquid for moulding in the fridge. Two level teaspoons will set the same amount of liquid to be spooned into serving glasses. Fruit purées and ingredients of a similar consistency, such as moulds and mousses, need 1 level teaspoon per ½ pint/ 300 ml purée for setting in glasses.

Hot weather affects gelatine, so allow a little extra to compensate. Similarly, if a tall or complicated mould is used, allow extra gelatine to give a firmer set.

*Some fresh fruit, such as pineapple, contain enzymes which prevent gelatine from working. However, these enzymes are destroyed in cooked and canned fruit, so they can be used in jellies.

Basic Recipes

Pastries

The pastries used in the recipes are not difficult. They can be made by hand or in a food mixer — the cutting action of a food processor is especially good for pastry. Butter is recommended for its fine flavour but, for the basic shortcrust, a mixture of yellow and white fats is best. Do not use soft tub fats or reduced fat butters. If making pastry by hand, remove the butter from the fridge ½ hour beforehand. If using a machine, use fats directly from the fridge.

Shortcrust Pastry

This is the general purpose pastry most often used for pies and tarts. Keep everything cool when making pastry, handle as little as possible and chill for 20-30 minutes before rolling.

> 9 oz/250g/heaped 2 cups plain (all-purpose) flour
> 4½ oz/125g/1 stick + 1 US tbsp butter, or half butter and half white fat
> 2 fl oz/50 ml/¼ cup very cold water

Weigh and measure ingredients accurately. Sift the flour into a large bowl. Add the butter and cut into small pieces. Rub butter into flour with finger tips. If using a pastry blender, lift the mixture as much as possible to aerate. Add chilled water. Mix with a knife or fork until the mixture clings together, then turn onto a floured worktop. Knead lightly once or twice until smooth. Wrap in greaseproof/waxed paper or foil and leave in the fridge to relax for 20 minutes before using.

Sweet Flan Pastry

This richer, sweet version of shortcrust pastry is the very light, crisp pastry used for open fruit tarts. This is the classic hand-made method.

> 9 oz/250g/heaped 2 cups plain (all-purpose) flour
> 4½ oz/125g/1 stick + 1 US tbsp butter
> 2½ oz/60g/2½ US tbsp caster (superfine) sugar
> l egg or 2 yolks, beaten
> 2 tsp/2½ US tsp lemon juice (or water)

Weigh ingredients accurately. Sift the flour into a bowl. Cut butte into small pieces and rub lightly into the flour, incorporating as much air as possible. Add the sugar and mix well. Make a well in the centre, then add the beaten egg and lemon juice. Mix with a knife until the dough clings together. Chill.

One-stage (Fork) Pastry

A smooth, slightly sweetened pastry. Exceptionally easy to handle and cooks to a light, crisp golden-brown.

8 oz/225g/2 sticks butter or block margarine, at room temperature
12 oz/350g/3 cups plain (all-purpose) flour
3 tbsp/3¾ US tbsp very cold water
1 oz/25g/scant ¼ cup icing (confectioners') sugar

Put the butter or margarine into a bowl, along with half the flour and all the water. Cream with a fork until thoroughly mixed. Sift together the remaining flour and icing/confectioners' sugar and, still using a fork, gradually work into the mixture to form a manageable dough. Turn out onto a floured work surface and knead lightly until smooth. Wrap in clingfilm and chill for ½ hour before use.

Magimix Sweet Pastry

This simple pastry is a favourite recipe. Sift 12 oz/350g/3 cups flour and a pinch of salt into the bowl of a food processor. Add 8 oz/225g/2 sticks cubed butter and process for about 15 seconds, until the mixture looks like breadcrumbs. Add 3 egg yolks and 3 oz/75g/3 US tbsp caster/superfine sugar and process for another 20 seconds, until the pastry clings together and forms a ball. Knead lightly to form a smooth dough. Wrap the ball in clingfilm and chill before use. Keeps for several days in the fridge and freezes well.

Rough Puff Pastry

This is easier than making home-made puff pastry and much nicer than the bought variety. It's the cold air which is folded into the pastry which acts as a raising agent and makes it very light. Equally good for sweet and savoury dishes.

8 oz/225g/2 cups plain (all-purpose) flour
½ tsp salt
few drops of lemon juice
4-6 oz/100-175g/1-1½ sticks unsalted butter
cold water

Sift the flour and salt into a bowl. Add the lemon juice and the butter, broken into pieces the size of a walnut. Add enough cold water to bind the ingredients. Turn onto a floured board and roll the pastry into a long strip. Fold it into three and press the edges together. Half-turn the pastry and rib it with the rolling pin to equalise the air in it and roll again into a strip. Fold in three, and repeat this until the pastry has had four rolls, folds and half-turns. It is then ready for use.
Note: Half fat to flour is the basic recipe, although three-quarters makes a richer pastry.

Icings

Almond Paste

For top and sides of an 8"/20 cm round or 7"/18 cm square cake. This is a moderate amount — almond paste addicts should double the quantities for a deep layer.

> 12 oz/350g/scant 2 cups ground almonds
> 6 oz/175g/1⅓ cups icing (confectioners') sugar, sifted
> 6 oz/175g/6 US tbsp caster (superfine) sugar, sifted
> 2 tsp lemon juice
> a few drops of natural almond essence
> 1 tbsp golden or navy rum (optional)
> 1 standard egg

Mix ground almonds with sifted sugars. Blend together lemon juice, almond essence and rum. Add to the almond mixture, together with enough egg to mix to a smooth paste. (This is very quickly and easily done in a Kenwood mixer.)

Gather together with the fingers and turn onto a work surface which has been dusted with icing/confectioners' sugar. Knead until smooth. Cut off about ⅓ of the ball and roll out to fit the sides of the cake, using a piece of string as a guide for the length and width of the strip.

Brush the sides of the cake with warmed apricot jam or lightly beaten egg white and apply the almond paste in two strips, blending the joins with the fingers.

Roll out the remaining almond paste to fit the top of the cake — this is easily done using the cake tin and string as guides. Brush the top of the cake with warmed apricot jam and invert onto the rolled-out almond paste. Press down gently but firmly to stick it in place. Work around the top edge with a palette knife to make a neat join. Use a straight-edged glass to roll around the outside of the cake, sticking the almond paste on firmly and giving a clean line. Leave cake upside down overnight. Next day, put right way up, cover lightly with tissue and leave for at least a day to dry out a little before icing.

White Christmas Icing (Royal Icing)

A softer, lighter version of the traditional Royal Icing. The glycerine (available from chemists) will keep the icing from becoming brittle, but if you like it firm on the outside and still fairly soft underneath, don't make the icing until a few days before Christmas. More lemon juice can be added for extra flavour if you like, but it tends to make the icing harden in storage, so extra glycerine may be needed

> 2 egg whites, whisked
> about 1 lb/450g/3½ cups icing (confectioners') sugar, sifted
> 2 tsp/2½ US tsp lemon juice
> 2 tsp/2½ US tsp glycerine

Whisk the egg whites lightly in a large bowl. Work about half of the sifted icing/confectioners' sugar into the egg whites, along with the lemon juice and glycerine. Gradually work in enough of the remaining sugar until the icing is thick enough to coat the back of a spoon without running off. Spread roughly over the top and sides of the cake, then flick into peaks. Decorate simply with a few sprigs of holly or other seasonal decoration. When the icing is dry, tie a red satin ribbon around the cake and finish with a double bow.

Vanilla Butter Icing

3 oz/75g/¾ stick butter, at room temperature
4 oz/100g/¾ cup icing (confectioners') sugar
vanilla essence

Cream the butter. Gradually add the sifted sugar and beat well until smooth and creamy. Add a few drops of vanilla essence and blend.

Chocolate Butter Icing

½ tsp coffee essence
l level tbsp/1¼ US tbsp cocoa powder
1 tbsp/1¼ US tbsp hot water
2 oz/50g/½ stick butter, at room temperature
4 oz/100g/¾ cup icing (confectioners') sugar

Put the coffee essence, cocoa and hot water into a cup or small bowl and mix well until smooth. Cream the butter and gradually work in the sifted sugar. Beat until smooth and creamy, then add the cocoa mixture.

Glacé Icing

6 ½ oz/200g/1 ⅓ cups icing (confectioners') sugar
6-7 tbsp/90-105 ml water
½ tsp vanilla essence

Sift the icing sugar into a bowl and mix in enough water to make a soft paste. Flavour with the vanilla (or other preferred favouring).

Variation

For lemon or orange flavoured icings, replace the water with juice and omit the vanilla.

Index

A

almonds
  Almond Paste, 127
  Cherry & Almond Buns, 35-6
  Frangipane Tart, 90
  Gingerbread Buns, 35
  Lemon Brûlée in an Almond Tart, 91-2
  Macaroons, 105
American banana bread, 37
apples
  Apple & Oatmeal Layer Cake, 95-6
  Apple Fadge, 21
  Blackberry & Apple Crumble, 95
  Blackberry & Apple Pie, 93
  Hilton Park Pancakes with Apples
    & Honey, 24-5
  Irish Apple Cake, 67
  Pancakes with Apple & Ginger
    Marmalade, 22-3
  Rhubarb & Crab-apple Crumble, 88-9
Ashford Castle Brown Bread, 7
Asparagus & Cashew Strudel with Port Wine
  Sauce, 87

B

baguettes
  Erriseask Baguettes, 44-5
Ballylickey Wheaten Bread, 5
Ballylickey Yummy Cake, 74-5
Ballymaloe Walnut Meringue, 116
banana bread
  American, 37
  Cashel House, 36-7
  Whole-wheat, 38
Barbara's Guinness 'Yeast' Bread, 64
barbecue garlic & herb bread, 58
barm brack, 29
  Hallowe'en Barm Brack, 110-11
Basic White Yeast Dough, 47
Bee's Brown Bread, 4
bicarbonate of soda, 2
biscuits, 77-81
  for cheese, 79-81
  Easter biscuits, 109-10
  Enniscoe Oatmeal Biscuits with Curry Powder,
    80
  Ginger Biscuits, 78
  Glassdrumman Flapjacks, 77

Macaroons, 105
Plain Oatmeal Biscuits, 79
Rich Chocolate Cookies, 78
Shortbread Fingers, 79
Star Biscuits, 106
Water Biscuits, 81
Wheaten Biscuits, 77
Wholemeal Biscuits, 80
blackberries
  Blackberry & Apple Crumble, 95
  Blackberry & Apple Pie, 94
Blue Haven Brown Bread, 52
Boiled Fruit Cake, 69
Bow Hall Muffins, 62-3
Boxty, 21-2
breads, 3-10
Brown Bread Ice Cream, 91
Brown Bread with Olive Oil, 44
Brown Yeast Bread with Mixed Grains, 50
buns
  Cherry & Almond Buns, 35-6
  Hot Cross Buns, 107-8
  Raspberry Buns, 36
buttermilk, 2, 3
  Buttermilk Cake, 32
  Buttermilk Griddle Scones, 24
  Buttermilk Scones, 12

C
cakes, 65-76. *See also* Tea Breads
  Ballylickey Yummy Cake, 74-5
  Boiled Fruit Cake, 69-70
  Caragh Lodge Wedding Cake, 111-13
  Carrot Cake, 75-6
  Cherry Cake, 66-7
  Christmas Cake, 100-1
  Chocolate Hazelnut Cake, 73
  Crunchy Date Cake, 76
  Dried Fruit Cake, 68
  Gur Cake, 70-1
  Irish Apple Cake, 67
  Irish Coffee Cake, 72
  Irish Whiskey Cake, 71-2
  Light Cherry Cake, 33
  Porter Cake, 31, 68-9
  Seed Cake, 66
  Simnel Cake, 108-9
  Sponge Layer Gâteau, 74
Caragh Lodge Onion Bread, 56
Caragh Lodge Wedding Cake,
  111-13
Caramel Topping, 114

carrots
  Carrot & Sultana Scones, 15-16
  Carrot Cake, 75-6
Cashel House Banana Bread, 36-7
cashews
  Asparagus & Cashew Strudel
  with Port Wine Sauce, 87
cheese, 1
  biscuits for, 79-81
  Cheese Bread, 47
  Rathsallagh Tomato & Cheese
    Bread, 55
  Traditional Cheese Scones, 12
cheesecake
  Gaby's Cheesecake, 96
cherries
  Cherry & Almond Buns, 35-6
  Cherry Cake, 66-7
  Light Cherry Cake, 33
chocolate
  Chocolate Butter Icing, 128
  Chocolate Fudge Terrine, 113-14
  Chocolate Hazelnut Cake, 73
  Chocolate Swiss Roll. *See* Yule Log
  Rich Chocolate Cookies, 78
Christmas baking, 97-105
  Christmas biscuits, 105-6
  mince pies, 104-5
  Mincemeat Lattice Pie, 104-5
  Mincemeat Tarts with
    Streusel Topping, 103
  Mincemeat with Irish Whiskey, 102-3
  Quick Christmas Cake with
    Glazed Fruit & Nut Topping,
    100-1
  Traditional Christmas Pudding, 98-9
  White Christmas Icing, 127
  Yule Log, 101-2
Cider Brack, 31
Clohamon Scones, 14
Clonbrook Breakfast Scones, 28
coffee
  Irish Coffee Cake, 72
Continental Fruit Bread, 60
cookies. *See* biscuits
Coopershill Wholemeal Bread, 43
cream of tartar, 3
crêpes. *See* pancakes
Crookedwood House Wholemeal Loaf,
  48-9
Crunchy Date Cake, 76
curry powder

Enniscoe Oatmeal Biscuits with
    Curry Powder, 80

D
dates
  Crunchy Date Cake, 76
  Date Cake, 32
  Date and Walnut Loaf, 39
  Date Loaf, 37
desserts, 113-18. *see also* puddings
  Amaretti Dacquoise, 117
  Ballymaloe Walnut Meringue, 116
  Chocolate Fudge Terrine, 113-14
  Profiteroles with Caramel Topping,
    114-15
  Snow Roll with Lemon Curd, 115-16
  Strawberry Kirsch Cake, 118
Dingle Pies, 83
dried fruits, 119-20
  Boiled Fruit Cake, 69-70
  Caragh Lodge Wedding Cake, 111-3
  Christmas Cake, 100-1
  Dried Fruit Cake, 68
  Gur Cake, 70
  mince pies, 104-5
  Mincemeat Lattice Pie, 104-5
  Mincemeat Tarts with Streusel Topping, 103
  Mincemeat with Irish Whiskey, 102
  Traditional Christmas Pudding, 98-9
dumplings
  Boxty Dumplings, 22

E
Easter, 107-10
  Easter biscuits, 109-10
  Hot Cross Buns, 107-8
  Simnel Cake, 108-9
Enniscoe Oatmeal Biscuits with Curry Powder,
  80
Erriseask Baguettes, 44-5

F
Fadge, 21
flapjacks
  Glassdrumman Flapjacks, 77
flour, 1, 122-3
Flower Crêpes with Summer Berry Filling, 25
Frangipane Tart, 90
fruit breads
  Continental Fruit Bread, 60
fruit cakes, 68-71
Fruit Soda Bread, 30

G
garlic
  BBQ Garlic & Herb Pulled
    Bread, 58
  Garlic Bread, 47
gelatine, 124
ginger
  Ginger Biscuits, 78
  Gingerbread Buns, 35
  Hunter's Ginger Cake, 34
  Oatmeal Gingerbread, 34
  Traditional Gingerbread, 33
Glassdrumman Flapjacks, 77
gooseberries
  Rhubarb & Gooseberry Pie, 94
griddle baking, 18-28
  Apple Fadge, 21
  Boxty, 21-2
  Boxty Dumplings, 22
  Boxty Pancakes, 22
  Buttermilk Griddle Scones, 24
  Clonbrook Breakfast Scones, 28
  Flower Crêpes with Summer Berry
    Filling, 25-6
  Hot Drop Pancakes, 26-7
  Hunter's Drop Scones, 26
  Lacken House Potato Cakes, 20-1
  Longueville Potato Cakes, 23
  Oatcakes, 19
  Oatmeal Pancakes, 20
  Pratie Oaten, 19
  Roundwood House Griddle Scones, 28
  Soda Farls, 27
Guinness
  Barbara's Guinness 'Yeast' Bread, 64
  Boiled Fruit Cake, 69-70
Gur Cake, 70-1

H
Hallowe'en, 110-11
hazelnuts, 122
  Chocolate Hazelnut Cake, 73
herbs
  BBQ Garlic & Herb Pulled Bread, 58
  Herb Bread, 47
Hilton Park Pancakes with Apples
    & Honey, 24-5
Hot Cross Buns, 107
Hot Drop Pancakes, 26
Hunter's Drop Scones, 26
Hunter's Ginger Cake, 34

I
ice cream
  Brown Bread Ice Cream, 91
icing, 127-8
  Chocolate Butter Icing, 128
  Glace Icing, 128
  Vanilla Butter Icing, 128
  White Christmas Icing, 127
Indian Meal Scones, 17
Irish Apple Cake, 67
Irish-American Soda Bread, 63
Irish Coffee Cake, 72
Irish Tea Cake, 31
Irish Whiskey Cake, 71-2
Irwin, Florence, 2

K
kirsch
  Strawberry Kirsch Cake, 118

L
Lacken House potato cakes, 20-1
lemons
  Lemon Brûlée in an Almond Tart, 91-2
  lemon curd, 115
  Lemon Tart, 92
Light White Yeast Bread, 54
Longueville Potato Cakes, 23
Lovett's White Soda Bread, 9

M
macaroons, 105
marigolds
  Old Rectory Marigold &
    Parsley Bread, 59
Marmalade Muffins, 62
marzipan, 108-9
Max's Brown Bread, 49
meat pies, 83-5
Mighty White Dough, 42
milk, souring, 3
mincemeat
  mince pies, 104-5
  Mincemeat Lattice Pie, 104-5
  Mincemeat Tarts with Streusel
    Topping, 103
  Mincemeat with Irish Whiskey, 102
Mitchell's Brown Soda Bread with Seeds, 9-10
Moyglare Yeast Bread, 42
muffins
  Bow Hall Muffins, 62-3
  Marmalade Muffins, 62

N
Newport House Brown Bread, 6
nuts, 121-2. see also almonds; cashews;
  hazelnuts; walnuts

O
oatmeal
  Apple & Oatmeal Layer Cake, 95-6
  Enniscoe Oatmeal Biscuits with
    Curry Powder, 80
  Oatcakes, 19
  Oatmeal Pancakes, 20
  Oatmeal Scones, 13
  Plain Oatmeal Biscuits, 79
  Pratie Oaten, 20
Old Rectory Marigold & Parsley Bread,
  59
olive oil
  Brown Bread with Olive Oil, 44
  White Bread with Olive Oil &
    Poppy Seeds, 56-7
Olive Rolls, 61
Onion Bread, 56

P
pancakes
  Boxty Pancakes, 22
  Buttermilk Pancakes, 107
  Flower Crêpes with Summer
    Berry Filling, 25-6
  Hilton Park Pancakes with Apples &
    Honey, 24-5
  Hot Drop Pancakes, 26-7
  Oatmeal Pancakes, 20
  Pancakes with Apple & Ginger
    Marmalade, 22-3
parsley
  Old Rectory Marigold & Parsley
    Bread, 59
pastry, 82-96, 125-6
  Asparagus & Cashew Strudel
    with Port Wine Sauce, 87
  Beefsteak & Kidney Pie with
    Suet Crust, 84-5
  Dingle Pies, 83
  Lemon Brûlée in an Almond
    Tart, 91
  Lemon Tart, 92
  Magimix Sweet Pastry, 126
  Mince Pies, 103-4
  one-stage pastry, 126
  Rhubarb & Gooseberry Pie, 94

rough puff pastry, 126
shortcrust pastry, 125
Spinach & Cheese Flan, 86
Steak & Oyster Pie, 84
Sweet Flan Pastry, 125
pizza base, 54
Plain Oatmeal Biscuits, 79
Port Wine Sauce, 87
Porter Cake, 31, 68-9
potatoes
  Boxty, 21-2
  Lacken House Potato Cakes, 20-1
  Longueville Potato Cakes, 23
  Oven-baked Potato Cakes, 13
  Pratie Oaten, 19
praline, 117
puddings, 88-96. *see also* desserts
  Apple & Oatmeal Layer Cake, 95-6
  Blackberry & Apple Crumble, 95
  Blackberry & Apple Pie, 93
  Brown Bread Ice Cream, 91
  Frangipane Tart, 90
  Gaby's Cheesecake, 96
  Lemon Brûlée in an Almond Tart, 91-2
  Lemon Tart, 92
  mince pies, 104-5
  Mincemeat Lattice Pie, 104-5
  Mincemeat Tarts with Streusel
    Topping, 103
  Mincemeat with Irish Whiskey, 102
  Rhubarb & Cinnamon Tart, 88
  Rhubarb & Crab-apple Crumble, 88-9
  Rhubarb & Gooseberry Pie, 94
  Rhubarb Soufflé Tart, 89-90
  Traditional Christmas Pudding, 98-9

Q
Quay House Flat Bread, 54-5
Quick & Easy Whole-wheat Bread, 45

R
raising agents, 123-4
Raspberry Buns, 36
Rathsallagh Tomato & Cheese Bread, 55
rhubarb
  Rhubarb & Cinnamon Tart, 88
  Rhubarb & Crab-apple Crumble, 88-9
  Rhubarb & Gooseberry Pie, 94
  Rhubarb Soufflé Tart, 89-90
Roundwood House Griddle Scones, 28
Rye Bread, 57

S
St Ernans Mixed Grain & Yogurt Loaf, 8
scones, 11-17
  Butter Scones, 15
  Buttermilk Griddle Scones, 24
  Buttermilk Scones, 12
  Carrot & Sultana Scones, 15-16
  Clohamon Scones, 14
  Clonbrook Breakfast Scones, 28
  Fruit Scones, 11
  Indian Meal Scones, 17
  James's Scones, 16
  Oatmeal Scones, 13
  Oven-baked Potato Cakes, 13
  Spicy Fruit Scones, 16-17
  Traditional Cheese Scones, 12
  Traditional Plain Scones, 11
  Traditional Rich Tea Scones, 11
seeds
  Mitchell's Brown Soda Bread with Seeds, 9-10
  Seed Cake, 66
  White Bread with Olive Oil & Poppy Seeds, 56-7
Shamrock Foods, 119-24
Shortbread Fingers, 79
Shrove Tuesday, 106-7
Snow Roll with Lemon Curd, 115-6
soda breads, 1
  Ashford Castle Brown Bread, 7
  Ballylickey Wheaten Bread, 5
  Basic Brown Soda Bread, 4
  Bee's Brown Bread, 4
  Fruit Soda Bread, 30
  Grandmother's Bread, 5
  Granny Nixon's Wheaten Loaf, 6
  Irish-American Soda Bread, 63
  Ken Buggy's Famous Brown Bread, 10
  Lovett's White Soda Bread, 9
  Mary Ann's Brown Bread, 7
  Mitchell's Brown Soda Bread with Seeds, 9-10
  Newport House Brown Bread, 6
  St Ernans Mixed Grain & Yogurt Loaf, 8
  Wheaten Bread, 8-9
soda farls, 27
speciality breads, 53-64
  Barbara's Guinness 'Yeast' Bread, 64
  BBQ Garlic & Herb Pulled Bread, 58
  Bow Hall Muffins, 62-3
  Continental Fruit Bread, 60
  Irish-American Soda Bread, 63
  Light White Yeast Bread, 54
  Marmalade Muffins, 62

Old Rectory Marigold & Parsley Bread, 59
Olive Rolls, 61
Onion Bread, 56
Quay House Flat Bread, 54-5
Rathsallagh Tomato & Cheese Bread, 55
Temple House Rye Bread, 57
Walnut Bread, 61
White Bread with Olive Oil & Poppy Seeds, 56-7
Spinach & Cheese Flan, 86
Sponge Layer Gâteau, 74
Star Biscuits, 106
Strawberry Kirsch Cake, 118
Streusel Topping, 103
Suet Pastry, 84-5
sugar, 120-1

T
tea breads, 29-34
  Buttermilk Cake, 32
  Date Cake, 32-3
  Fruit Soda Bread, 30
  Hunter's Ginger Cake, 34
  Irish Tea Cake, 31
  Oatmeal Gingerbread, 34
  Tea Brack, 30-1
  Traditional Gingerbread, 33
  Whiskey Brack, 31
Temple House Rye Bread, 57
tomatoes
  Rathsallagh Tomato & Cheese Bread, 55
Traditional Gingerbread, 33
Treacle Bread, 49

W
walnuts, 122
  Ballymaloe Walnut Meringue, 116
  Date & Walnut Loaf, 39
  Walnut Bread, 61
Water Biscuits, 81
wedding cake, 111-13
Wheaten Biscuits, 77
whiskey
  Irish Coffee Cake, 72
  Irish Whiskey Cake, 71
  Mincemeat with Irish Whiskey, 102-3
  Whiskey Brack, 31
White Bread with Olive Oil & Poppy Seeds, 56-7
Wholemeal
  Biscuits, 80
  Coopershill Bread, 43
  Health Bread, 51
  Quick Yeast Bread, 46-7

Wholewheat
  Banana Bread, 38
  Quick & Easy Whole-wheat
    Bread, 45-6

Y
yeast breads, 40-52
  basic white yeast dough, 47
  BBQ Garlic & Herb Pulled Bread, 58
  Blue Haven Health Bread, 52
  Brown Bread with Olive Oil, 44
  Brown Yeast Bread with
    Mixed Grains, 50
  Caragh Lodge Onion Bread, 56
  Continental Fruit Bread, 60
  Coopershill Wholemeal Bread, 43
  Crookedwood House
    Wholemeal Loaf, 48-9
  Erriseask Baguettes, 44-5
  Light White Yeast Bread, 54
  Malty Brown Bread, 48
  Max's Brown Bread, 49-50
  Mighty White Dough, 42-3
  Moyglare Yeast Bread, 42
  Olive Rolls, 61
  Quick & Easy Whole-wheat
    Bread, 45-6
  Quick Wholemeal Yeast Bread, 46-7
  Rathsallagh Tomato & Cheese
    Bread, 55
  Temple House Rye Bread, 57
  Treacle Bread, 49
  Walnut Bread, 61
  White Bread with Olive Oil
    & Poppy Seeds, 56-7
  Wholemeal Health Bread, 51
yellow meal, 2
yogurt, 3
  St Ernans Mixed Grain
    & Yogurt Loaf, 8
  Yogurt Loaf, 38
Yule Log, 101-2